van Leonidov

Introduction by Vieri Quilici
Essay by S.O. Khan-Magomedov

Catalogue 8

Published by the Institute for
Architecture and Urban Studies and
Rizzoli International Publications, Inc.

Contents

Editors
Kenneth Frampton
Silvia Kolbowski

Managing Editors
Silvia Kolbowski
Laura Bell

Designer
Massimo Vignelli

Design Coordinator
Abigail Moseley

Editorial Consultant
Joan Ockman

Production
Patricia Bates
Marguerite McGoldrick

**IAUS Exhibition
Catalogues Program
Co-Directors**
Kenneth Frampton
Silvia Kolbowski

**Leonidov Exhibition
Program Director**
Andrew MacNair

Exhibition Curator
Gerritt Oorthuys

Exhibition Coordinator
William Eitner

First published in the United States of
America in 1981 by Rizzoli International
Publications, Inc. 712 Fifth Avenue,
New York, N.Y. 10019

© The Institute for Architecture
and Urban Studies
8 West 40th Street
New York, N.Y. 10018

Typography by Myrel Chernick
Printed by Morgan Press, Inc.

Preface

Kenneth Frampton

There is probably no figure of the Modern Movement who haunts the stage of the twentieth century with such persistence as Ivan Leonidov. Once captured, the imagination can never quite rid itself of the appeal of these vague and provocative drawings, these projective icons and schematic plans for hypothetical ahistorical worlds. However familiar they become, the magic of these images endures—the subtle poetry of some scant lines and colorless but iridescent renderings; a montage contaminated by the cinematic; a virgin landscape permeated by technology; an image which paradoxically evokes an infinite and passified universe as boundless as the sea. With Leonidov we confront a modernity that resists obsolescence; we encounter an architect who, despite his limited output, continues, after fifty years, to be prophetic in a way that undermines our received ideas of cultural transmutation and transmission.

Leonidov reminds us that the advent of modernity brought in its wake an epistemological break which neither the species being nor its art can escape. In Leonidov's hedonist, socialist world, the loss of iconology is mediated by nature and technique. And while his work remains embedded in representation, it is a universe in which representation *in se* can hardly be said to exist. Nothing seems to obtain in this world save the courageous unfolding of energy—the *élan vital* of the species flying toward its heroic destiny; a paradoxical Suprematist teleology which insists that nothing exists apart from this flight.

Where in the unfolding trajectory of a neo-technological world do we not find the fragmentary typology of Leonidov's utopia: from Santos Dumont's airship of 1901 to R. Buckminster Fuller's Dymaxion Home of 1927, from Mies Van der Rohe at his most ephemeral in 1922 (patently influenced by Malevich), to SOM's Marine Gunnery School built at Great Lakes, Illinois, in 1954. At their most ephemeral Leonidov's projects are not so much designed as they are posited; a geodesic dome here or a glazed pyramid there, set amid tropical verdure—an *architecture degree-zero* whose liberative intent transcends the culture of *tectonic* form. Thus, between the family that is too small and the tribe that is too big, there is in Leonidov's projections for *Dom-Kommuna* the implication of a liberative communality. His Magnitogorsk collective dwelling implies a set of interpersonal associations that are changing, a cellular solitude whose mediating condition is the limited social unit within which it is contained. There is in this gymnasium-*cum*-cafe terrace, the strong suggestion of a ludic lifestyle, wherein an everyday spontaneity would be free to escape from the confines of a cruciform winter garden into the Edenic landscape of a neon-lit, Erasian night.

Yet despite the erotic and liberative dimensions suggested by this vision, Leonidov's architecture remains grounded in the paradigms of the eighteenth- and nineteenth-century avant garde, that is to say, in pure geometry and pure technique as the arbiters of architectural form. At its most avant-garde, his works project a supra-tectonic, an "almost nothing" that attains its non-rhetorical apotheosis in its implied detachment from the earth. Of this El Lissitzky wrote in 1930, "The idea of the conquest of the substructure, the earthbound, can be extended even further and calls for the conquest of gravity as such. It demands floating structures, and physical—dynamic architecture." In his later, more traditional vein, however, Leonidov turned toward the naive earthiness of the Russian icon, toward a kind of *zaumy* (transrational) Piranesian method of combining the old with the new—the towers of the Kremlin with the silos of the Narkomtiazhprom.

No more apt testament perhaps can be made to the pervasiveness of Leonidov's influence than that the initiators of this exhibition have in themselves been directly touched by this Russian master—above all the Dutch architects Gerrit Oorthuys and Rem Koolhaas, Koolhaas publicly declaring his affinity for neo-Suprematism in his entry for the Centre Pompidou competition of 1973. From this initial bridgehead, the extraordinarily rich work of OMA has gradually evolved: the iconic projects of Koolhaas, Elia and Zoe Zenghelis, Madelon Vriesendorp, and, at some remove, Zahar Hadid.

Possibly none of this would have been achieved had it not been for the enthusiasm of Oorthuys and Koolhaas for the Soviet avant-garde, their numerous visits to Russia, their contact with Leonidov's heirs, and then, in 1977, Oorthuys's timely retrospective exhibition at the IAUS dedicated to the memory of an elusive modern master.

Introduction

Vieri Quilici
Translated by Stephen Sartarelli

Frontispiece. Group photograph of the OSA (Association of Contemporary Architects) Conference in Moscow, 1928.

1. *Gurevich*
2. *A. S. Nikol'sky*
3. *Victor Vesnin*
4. *Alexander Vesnin*
5. *R. Shilov*
6. *Alex Gan*
7. *M. Sinyavsky*
8. *Nabel'baum*
9. *Mal'ts*
10. *Kornfel'd*
11. *V. Kratyuk*
12. *R.I.A. Khiger*
13. *G. Vegman*
14. *Ivan Leonidov*
15. *Nina Vorotyntseva*
16. *V. Vladimirov*
17. *L. Slavina*
18. *T. Chizhikova*
19. *Nadyezhda Krasheninnikova*
20. *M. Gaken*
21. *M. Barshch*
22. *G. Orlov*
23. *I. Milinis*
24. *S. Levitan*
25. *Moisei Ginzburg*
26. *F. Yalovkin*
27. *N. Sokolov*

If one considers the history of Soviet architecture in terms of generations, it is clear that Ivan Leonidov belonged to a third generation of Constructivism, a generation completely indigenous to the 1920s, different and distinctly separate from the preceding ones—different from the first generation, which around 1920 was involved in the *objet d'art* currents of an essentially pictorial, figurative culture; and different from the second generation, which was identified with the various architectural groups which came into being around 1923 and thereafter. Those belonging to these generations had matured and consolidated their ideas in the pre-revolutionary phase of the artistic avant garde; that is, they had irreversibly compromised themselves with the past reality of the revolutionary years.

In Leonidov, instead, we encounter the *new man* produced by the cultural instruments that the Revolution had created for itself in the aftermath of October. Leonidov was a product of the *Vkhutemas* school, a totally original product of "technico-artistic" education, which was liberated from the past, from history, and based on the specificity and technique of specialized languages.

In this way the novelty of Leonidov's Lenin Institute project can be linked to the generational character of his work, while at the same time it is an iconic image, emblematic of the Soviet phase of Russian architecture then directed toward renewing certain themes and reorienting certain individuals. Just as Tatlin's Tower represents the initial avant-garde candidacy for the role of being the ideological medium of the Revolution, so the Lenin Institute seems to condense within itself a solid, faultless confidence in the novelty of a technological world in the process of formation. It was no accident that Moisei Ginzburg, in presenting this project in the pages of *Sovremennaya Arkhitectura,* attributed to Leonidov the function of "breaking away" from a "system of methods, plans and elements (which had) become of common and habitual usage (and which) at best resulted in a uniformity of method, at worst in a threat of stylistic banality." And since this comment would later become part of a comprehensive evaluation of the activities of the Organization of Contemporary Architects (OSA), drawn up on the occasion of the first exhibition of modern architecture (1927)—that is, at that delicate moment of critical reflection on Constructivism—it is clear that great hopes were placed in the new man, who had attained maturity after the Revolution and "whose education (was) entirely the product of the new regime."[1] These hopes were held by the representatives of the preceding generations, who were counting on a renewal of art, technique, and science, almost as a necessary result of an automatic historical progression.

What weighed most heavily on the Constructivists, what might be called the source of their constant sense of guilt, was the purely figurative, pictorial-object origin of their pursuits. Meanwhile, what had emerged as the architect's mission, his professional calling—authority in building and control of the urban scale—seemed to have been neglected in the work of the first two generations and the solutions to such problems postponed until better times.

Ginzburg maintained that it was precisely with Leonidov that the "renewal" came to involve "the very concept of building and of the city on which and in which this building may be erected." The "purely spatial architectonic solution" seems in this way to synthesize all the desires for renewal motivating and agitating Constructivism from within.

One cannot help but be struck by the "academic" judgment expressed by N.A. Ladovsky at Vkhutemas on the occasion of Leonidov's receipt of his "final diploma" awarded for his Lenin Institute project), in which he emphasized the "progressivist artistic culture" and the "love for technical conceptions: with which the project was "pervaded." For Ladovsky a positive judgment of this sort could have signified an admiration beyond his well-known interest in the rational use of technique, which was not so much structural as it was related to the representation of architectonic form (architecture judged by the rule of architecture). This positive judgment is all the more remarkable for coming from the most well-known representative of the formalist avant garde, who was himself impressed by the novelty of Leonidov's work.

What seems to characterize most the features of the *new man* is precisely this "love" for technique, which clearly is something more than an interest, more than a commitment to research and experimentation in the field of technique. It is a question of both predisposition and a commitment to assimilating the concrete events of an age in the process of rapid evolution, a matter of stressing the significance of a culture founded on structural principles.

The "construction of everyday life," of the *byt,* the way of life, which constituted the great ambition of the first Constructivists and especially those of *leftist* origin, now seemed to become an attainable goal, but only within the terms and limits of a consistent technical exploitation of the possibilities for realization. The materials for construction were to define the limits of the area within which the technician of the spatial-urban structure was supposed to operate (this technician being no longer expected to exorcise the world of objects or to mythify a culture of materials). The materials of construction were the "decisive factors in the determination of the style and the architectural composition in its entirely, together with the conditions of the society and the life in general."

The city, which had been seen predominantly as a field of action for the avant garde, the the *palette-square*—the space in which to mix the scarlet colors of subversive expression, the pathos of the years immediately following the Revolution—now seemed to give way to the city seen as a physical realm in which it was possible to extend, spread, and organize the objects produced on a large scale by the new technology (the "city on which and in which" to erect the building). The urban realm was to be recuperated through a completely different sense of spatiality, through a sense for the physical continuity of space. With Leonidov, space became the unifying element coordinating the centrifugal dynamism of the architectonic structures built, as a rule, on Cartesian axes, which were projected according to the exact geometry of the site.

There no longer existed the anguish of the single architectonic object, the isolated condensor of life, the sculpture on a large scale intended to strike the observer by its uniqueness, by the very unrepeatable quality of its own image suspended, as it were, in a void. The propaganda booths, the object-constructions and stagings in the Red Square or in front of the Winter Palace, Vladimir Tatlin's Tower reproduced in effigy and carried around in procession—all this formed part of the world of experiences for which the city, the urban space, was only the background or the shell that contained them. The city was merely a sphere in which to exercise the intentional and creative function of propaganda.

The *new man* believed in the city as he believed in nature. For architecture, extension in space constituted the natural condition of growth, while for the city the recuperation of nature implied the acquisition of an unlimited quantity of space available for its own structuring.

The city was seen as an assembly of topological units and spatial extensions. The units were individually characterized, discrete in their exact distribution, in their apparent isolation. And yet the vast topological space was defined by the natural and architectonic shapes themselves (it constituted their opposite or their complement), while the discrete units were projected into a comprehensive space that included them in so far as it governed them geometrically.

The result of this was a conception of the city as an infinite spatial whole, a conception of space as a non-material coagulant which was nevertheless endowed with a dimensionality of its own, a continuous potential for architectural formalization. It would seem that behind the confident placing of architectonic objects in urban space, one can already sense the tasks that architects would be asked to respond to after 1930, that is, the building of the new industrial cities of the expanding Five-Year-Plans. But Leonidov's early projects were not yet affected by any sort of political pressure; they are pure intellectual prescience, the fruit of a subjective interpretation of conditions which permitted broader, clearer experiences. The new man believed fundamentally in an extension of his own planning potential to the extreme limit of boundless natural spatiality, and he believed in technology as the material instrument of such extension.

There are other figures from the same generation of Soviet architects who, although less well known, such as A. Krutikov, T. Varenzow, etc., were also inclined to consider spatiality as a natural condition, a tendency to transfer planning from the sphere of the imaginary to the sphere of the cosmic. Such tendencies perhaps reveal something about a particular politico-cultural moment in the development of a whole stratum of intellectuals.

But apart from his situation at a critical transitional moment, was this *new man* Leonidov, like certain of his contemporaries, a product distinctly separate from the period of the avant garde? Was this confident attitude toward technique, this desire to transfer the spirituality of the imagination into the physicality of space extending to infinity—cosmic space, yet still attainable by technological means—was all this really a sign of the decline of the ideology, of the intellectual utopia characteristic of the avant gardes of the early 1920s?

We have already touched on the affinity in terms of image between the projects for the Tatlin Tower and the Lenin Institute. At this point we will not touch on either the techniques or the functions for which these architectural objects were intended—the first one a primitive object, the second a sophisticated assembly—but rather the symbolic aspects from which their politico-ideological connotations arise. For the technological world of the Lenin Institute is only an evoked world, a world as yet to be realized through utilitarian techniques, and its general connotations do not imply a content substantially different from that of the work of Tatlin or, for example, of Alexander Vesnin, Leonidov's mentor and "supporter."

Moreover, there is in the work of Vesnin an archetypal Constructivist project—the 1924 design for the *Leningradskaya Pravda*—in which a meaningful affinity with a work of Leonidov may be discerned, above all with Leonidov's project for the printing press of *Izvestia,* a Vkhutemas "proof of study" of 1926. Both projects take the common legacy of the figurative avant garde as their expressive basis, the refined skeletal, ascetic, linear, structural language whose origins lie in Productivist theatrical construction.

But there are two, fundamental and complementary features that characterize Leonidov and help us to place him in the unrepeatable history of the avant garde: on the one hand his personal ideology, which is permeated by an aspiration to the universal and on the other his unending search for an

6 autonomously perfect form. These are, as we can see, the typical themes of the early figurative avant garde, and one can easily discern in Leonidov's use of them direct references, not to mention indirect but profound analogies, to the thought and work of Kazimir Malevich.

Ideolgy underlies all of Leonidov's works, and it constitutes their utopian constant—a kind of uninterrupted discourse belonging to a sphere of idea-forms, in which the individual projects and their related images represent only an instance of partial verification. His universalism, formed of a blend of technological humanism and futurism, finds its most typical and fitting manifestations in an endless succession of themes ranging from the workers' club to designated places of intellectual labor, from the city seen as a model to hygienics and grandeur to monuments dedicated to universal history or to humanity in general. In the latter half of the 1920s the workers' club constituted the most visible, significant architectural breakthrough in the art of propaganda. The *paintbrush-streets* and the *palette-squares,* the propaganda trains and boats had been widespread in the years of the war: they had been the instruments of an unprecedented diffusion of revolutionary imagery and content. However, after this there necessarily followed a phase where more specific goals were paramount and the construction of an information system—a formative system—was centered, at least initially, around the work-place. This led to the debate over "social condensors" and corresponding research into the typology of the workers' club.

In these already mature years of Constructivism, there was a tendency to conceive of architectural needs and especially of the workers' club as opportunities to plan a microcosm in which the premitive velleities of object-art would be overcome and the demands for social involvement met. This tendency is clearly manifest in work of Melnikov, whose stature remains inchallenged in this field for his formal coherence and his ingenious and versatile application of compositional methods appropriate to the spirit of the age.

In Leonidov's hands, the theme of the social club seems to gain a wider conceptual meaning and horizon. The physical extension of the type appears to be coupled with a profound broadening of the nature of the project. Even the phrase "new type of social club" sounds like a manifesto, and the words "new type of social" send one back to the original Constructivist demand for *ziznestroenje,* for the construction of everyday life, which in turn can be traced back to the Futurists' interest in the *byt*—the way of life. This subject was broached in the OSA congress of 1929, at which Leonidov presented his work on his own initiative. This presentation revealed his twofold interest in this subject, on the one hand an architectural concern for the spatial implications of the type, on the other, a conceptual-ideological interest in its presumed representation of social needs.

For Leonidov, the club was a center for activating mass labor and controlling cultural labor. Political campaigns, educational activities, and informational exchange were to constitute the basic activities of the club, while libraries, laboratories, and museum sections would make up its services.

It is evident that the ultimate goal was to educate the workers in the formation of a social consciousness, a class consciousness to be developed through a concept of spatial organization. Clearly the social role of architecture would thereby be reestablished according to its original terms. A reemergent socialist humanism this insinuated itself anew into architectural ideology.

Intellectual labor was seen as a liberation and a release from physical labor, and Leonidov's choice of the social club is indicative of his interest in combining the organization of labor with an architectural hypothesis. Nothing could be more typically related to the themes cherished by the avant garde from the start than this genuine effort to impart a political edge to productive relations.

Form was not seen as consisting only of external appearances, but on the contrary was identified with the "organizational result and the functional interdependencies between operational aspects and built form." On the other hand it was understood that "only by starting from the processes of labor is it possible to organize the working day the workers' cultural growth and leisure." The link between form and the construction of everyday life was forged anew, in the classical terms of the work of such figures as Ginzburg, A. Gan, and the Productivists.

Thus everyday life came to be defined as a combination of working activity, cultural growth, and leisure, and it is the second term that decidedly prevails in Leonidov's work, so much so that he attempted to connect class experience with the emotions and feelings, and through these, to proceed to the "general organization of consciousness." The eye is a precise mechanism," maintained Leonidov at the OSA congress, "which transmits what is seen to the consciousness. The positive or negative coloration of visual sensations depends on the class experience of our consciousness, irrespective of whether it is individual or social." This concept is close to Ladovsky's teachings at the Vkhutemas, which attempted to establish a link between the processes of perception-representation and the ideological context.

Leonidov's connection with the avant garde became most explicit in his conception of a space for universal use, an idea which characterized both his social club projects and his subsequent (1930) Palace of Culture proposal. In the early 1920s the avant garde typically followed two parallel and complementary paths: on the one hand that of invention *(tectonics)* and on the other that of a methodical quest for communicative form through the expressive use of materials *(workmanship)*. The natural point of tangency between these two routes was the theater, a sort of *laboratory* in which to test the efficacy of such investigations. The theater was capable of creating a social space for itself without having to compete with the real universe. The biomechanics of V. Meyerhold, the strict formalism of A. Tairov, the complex expressivity of Vachtangov, the marvelous theatrical acrobatics and the cinema of the *FEKS* (the "Eccentric Actor's Factory"), the choral reenactments during the Revolution—all this had already created a theatrical tradition so rich as to constitute an autonomous experience separate from the real, a formal tradition endowed with a social context both individual and exclusive—and encompassing the spectator-actors of the public. It was complemented by the desire to establish a link, a point of contact, between the interior theatrical space and the outside, the possibility of integrating external elements testifying to an urban sociality. Thus walkways from the streets would cross the stage and processions of demonstrators would occasionally march past bearing political news, together with automobiles and the clownish characters drawn from the world of motorized capitalism.

It is natural that Leonidov would have been influenced by these experiments when designing the universal spaces of his social clubs and the Palace of Culture. And as the painter/designer Lissitzky and the architects Barkhin and Vachtangov had sought to define the theatrical space of Meyerhold, so did Leonidov confront the same theme. In this he followed the typical line of avant-garde research.

Leonidov's "love" for technique led him to experiment with a total, microcosmic space in a large room capable of housing mass action. He proposed using devices and instruments that would mechanically reproduce images in such a way as to achieve a panoramic, planetary vision. An editorial in *Stroitel'sstvo Moskvy* stated, "One of the fundamental objectives of the Piscator theater is to create the action in the midst of the spectators. Leonidov's project resolves this in a more complete and organic manner, whereby the action of the stage unfolds amid the spectators, combining with cinematic projections."

In Leonidov's theatrical space, the action was situated amid the spectators, and external reality was colored by flashes of light and bombarded with artificial images. With the aid of such technically advanced instruments, Leonidov evoked a technological world much like that projected in the Lenin Institute project, a world of exorcised objects, where the objects themselves were kept alive and aggressive as in the language and theatrical presentations of Mayakovsky. Such was Leonidov's link with the original avant garde, a bridge all the more significant since in 1929 and 1930, when the competitions for the Kharkov theater and the Palace of the Soviets were officially anounced, the design of theatrical space was becoming an institutionalized theme and research was being encouraged into a typology grounded in the traditional separate functions of staging—whether dramatical or political—and in the correct arrangement of the spectators, especially in terms of visibility and acoustics.

8 Leonidov expressed his ideas on the organization of labor in his 1929-1930 project for the House of Industry. According to the ethical and idealist principles by which he argued that labor is not "an unpleasant necessity but the constant goal of life," it was feasible to reduce labor to its "physical and psychic state" and to bring it to the point of "being entirely organized." Such organization would aim either at a "higher tone of life," through gymnastics, light, air, rest and nutrition, etc., or at greater "productivity in labor itself." Either way, intellectual labor, previously regarded as a rest from physical labor, was now defined as an opportunity to develop one's "tone of life." The construction of life became possible as a result through the planning of biological space, as a purely organizational potential lying beyond social conflicts and the harsh confrontations with the relations of production.

This biological dimension led to optimal individuation within a hierarchy of separate groups, where the smallest unit, consisting of a few people, guaranteed a state of equilibrium with regard to the collectivity.

This principle, already present in the House of Industry project, was further elaborated in the socialist city projected for Magnitogorsk in 1930. On this occasion Leonidov revealed his concept of architecture as a reflection of an organizational will and at the same time as an exorcism of or flight from reality.

Leonidov saw the collectivization of life that accompanied the first years of the Revolution as well as the experimental "Residential Communes" as an excessive reduction of the psychological and intellectual dimension of the individual. As far as he was concerned, it was preferable to organize into small collectives "in which the individual personality does not get lost but has the possibility to develop itself to the maximum degree and to communicate with everyone, by moving progressively from the smallest collective to the largest." If the social club was supposed to perfect the individual, uniting scientific labor with creative activity and artistic production with physical education, the place of residence should guarantee a functional relationship in which "work, leisure, and culture are organically joined."

In his 1929 project for a monument to Christopher Columbus, this universalistic ideology, translated into a conceptual internationalism, manifested itself in an unambiguous manner. The glass dome, the spiral ramp, the two towers more than 300 meters tall, were supposed to suggest the idea of a "condensor of all the successes resulting from world-wide development," while "the radio, the radio images, the airport, and the seaport unite the movement of world culture," where "scientific laboratories...the brains of the monument, actually open up the unexplored roads of interplanetary communication."

The abstractly confident internationalism, the exalted isolation of the cognitive moment, the physical isolation of the place in which a rational organization of life and consciousness would be possible—all of this projected into an interplanetary, cosmic reality and surrounded by the ocean is unmistakably the sign of Utopia, the total sign which meaningfully anticipates projects that Leonidov was to outline in the years after the war, in the dramatic years of hope that followed victory, in the years of desperate political retrenchment. From the "City of Friendship among Nations" conceived during the construction of the United Nations building and imagined as a complex of skyscrapers to be erected on an island, to the "City of the Sun," designed as a communist city of the future in whose nucleus—comprising various cultural and bureaucratic services—would have been suspended an enormous sphere of gold, symbol of the sun, a continuous link was forged with the realm of the imaginary. The glass sphere of the Lenin Institute, the domes of reinforced glass of the Christopher Columbus monument, the golden sphere of the "City of the Sun," all these form a continuum of ideological references and a set of allusions that require no further comment. Yet we must still investigate the second aspect of Leonidov's background, his unique formal research, which, as we have remarked, can be traced back to an important source within the avant garde, namely Malevich.

But first it is necessary to put into perspective, even if schematically, the Futurist/Suprematist legacy in Constructivist architecture. However exciting, Leonidov's undertaking seems desperate in that he sought to reconcile the culture of materials with an abstract-geometrical expressivity, which amounts to trying to reunite (after more than a decade and with a revolution in between) the paths of Tatlin and Malevich, which parted in 1915 at the time of the *Tramway V* and 0.10 exhibitions.

However, one should not presume that this question concerns Leonidov alone, for from this point of view his history coincides (or rather represents and qualifies) an entire movement. Indeed, it should not be forgotten that in 1927 A. Gan was speculating about the possibility of bringing Suprematist language back into the discipline of architectural design as the original avant-gardist formal patrimony which had now become not only available but also communicable. With this notion he denied the declaration contained in the second issue of *SA,* "Our certificate," according to which the appropriation of Constructivist guidelines by painters and theater people in the early 1920s supposedly had led to the degeneration and death of the programs.[2]

The meaning of materials, the iconic value of materials in construction—detectable in the immediate and apparent quality of the surface, in the optical and tactile sensations aroused by various combinations (a laying bare of process, taken to the extreme)—constituted the object of Tatlin's research. From the first counter-reliefs of 1915 onward, the Productivists' experiments with theatrical construction owed much to Tatlin. Thus, A. Rodchenko, V. Stepanova, A.A. Exter, L. Popova, and the Sternberg brothers, among others, only transformed into dynamic theatrical elements the iconology of materials of Tatlin's relief works by uniting the actors, vital elements reduced to mechanical robots, with structural and material elements rendered dynamic by their incontrollable inner will to automation.

In this there was also a discourse of forms used as essences, a predilection for gestural and elemental "laconic" figures, a laying bare of the very substance of expression, or rather of the process that lay at the base of the formal genesis of Constructivism and Formalism (I am thinking of the theme of *prem,* which was to become the nucleus of formalist theory and was connected with the theme of montage). Such "essentiality" was at once primitive and mechanized, and the use of conventional and symbolic forms was coupled with

mechanistic references and reverberations which tended toward the abstract-geometric: it is enough to think of the populist-Cubist of Malevich, the "conventional" theater of Meyerhold, the rigorously formal theater of Tairov (and, naturally, the importance of Symbolist roots in their experiences).

We have referred earlier to the grotesque and automatic theater of the *FEKS.* As we can tell from theatrical exhibitions and from early cinematographic works (*Oktjabrina),* these productions of the "Eccentric Actor's Factory" unequivocally belong to the period of the avant garde. They are surely of great import if we are to understand the Formalist outcome of the tendency toward *eccentricity* in the Russian Futurist movement. With the *FEKS,* as would happen later in an even more systematic way with Sergei Eisenstein, plot became process, that is, a reasoned calculation of the effects created by the association or succession of particularly pregnant, separate images—a calculation of expressibility based on montage.

There is little doubt that Ladovsky acted as the element of continuity between the prewar period of the avant garde and its post war development. His contribution to the Institute of Culture *(Inchuk)* and the Vkhutemas lay essentially in the systematization of those experimental elements in figurative art that had already become a kind of iconological legacy within the entire post-Cubist and generally Expressionist avant garde (see Ladovsky's own *dom-kommuna* and V. Krinsky's grandstand project. After the debate at the *(Inchuk)* in the winter of 1920-21, in which Kandinsky took part as the author of a program that foreshadowed his later contribution to the Weimar Bauhaus, the task of systematic education was transformed into a veritable theory of architecture, of architecture as architectonic form.

Thus, in order to understand the meaning and importance of Leonidov's language at its origin and his commitment to a modern architectural tendency that can be defined as abstract, and in order to uncover his evident connections to Corbusian volumetric Purism (it was Le Corbusier himself who recognized the important formal departures made by Leonidov while working on the Centrosoyuz), it is necessary

10   to go back to Ladovsky and his collaborators, who from 1919 on laid the foundations of a discipline which he himself defined as rational, in obvious allusion to the equally foundational work of Le Corbusier (who, incidentally, kept his own poetic intact).

Moreover, the recognition of Purism as a common point of reference—inasmuch as it was an attempt to extend systematically the analytical findings of Cubism—was made explicit by N. Dokuchayev, who in several essays sought to describe the lesson to be learned from Ladovsky. With the exception of a few extraordinary writings, such as the famous text on the practice of formal representation at the Vkhutemas in 1920, Ladovsky left no direct testimony of his teachings.

But it is also necessary to go back to the figure of Melnikov. It was in fact a similar formalism that caused him to join Ladovsky's ASNOVA group and later to participate in the OSA exhibition, which even more clearly followed the Formalist technique of montage.

Montage should also be considered to have influenced the architectural syntax of Leonidov. The formalism of Melnikov seems to transfer the Shlovskian principle of the *ostranenie* correctly into architecture by means of its montage of materials originating in everyday reality. This principle was taken to its extreme lengths by Melnikov, to the point of kitsch, Melnikov's miscellaneous references being occasionally modernistic, occasionally pseudo-Classical, evasive, etc.; they were inferred from a world, from a reality, that at bottom was profoundly heterogeneous.

On the other hand, Leonidov's formalism was more rarefied, more figuratively and definitively abstract (it did not arise out of analogies of references to objects, as was the case with Melnikov or Golosov), but instead from the assumption of the geometric figure as its fundamental semantic unit. Individual architectonic volumes remain detached from one another; they are discrete units separated by rarefied spaces, by particularly tense and meaningful voids. Nevertheless, the matching or counterposition of the individual elements still remains a variation of the principle of montage; it is perhaps more subtle, more oblique, less obvious and mechanical than that of Melnikov, but nevertheless related to it.

Moreover, even in the matching of the essential (the "laconism" of volume and material usually extended over a large, even surface) with the accidental or the accessory (the technological detail defined on a decidedly inferior scale), the change in scale only serves to isolate and stress the two aspects, once again according with the principle of distancing as applied to two senses: the general exalting the particular, and the particular unveiling the general in a new light. "All the grandeur of the sea," wrote Leonidov, "is unveiled through a form measured against man (like a shrub, for example)."

It is clear, in any case, that the experiments of Melnikov and Leonidov relied on the same belief in the usefulness of an aggregational-compositional method of a conventional type, a method reducible to general principle, to formal typologies, and unlike the tendency of a manneristic Constructivism which in the later 1920s aimed at reducing itself to a form of empirical and handbook functionalism (as Ginzburg himself pointed out when he called attention to the "system of methods, plan, and elements which have become of common usage"). On the other hand, the experiments of Leonidov and Melnikov were not unlike the possibly more primitive but more authentic Constructivism practiced by someone like A. Vesnin who, as we have seen, was recognized by Leonidov as a master.

Moreover, we should not be misled by the seeming contradiction between the Formalist nature of Leonidov's architecture and the choice of sides that he took by adhering to the OSA and not the ASNOVA, the latter being the side to which he should logically have belonged (as with El Lissitzky, who was another key figure in the integration of avant-garde experimentation in figurative art into the architecture-planning field and who in 1926, upon his return to the U.S.S.R. collaborated with Ladovsky). In reality, as many have often maintained, the relations between the Constructivist-Productivist camp and the Formalist camp were so extensive and of such a nature that, beyond the often bitter polemics that divided the two camps, one can say that there existed a substantial affinity of interests between the two, especially formal interests.[3]

It was precisely through Vesnin that Leonidov sought to ally himself with the tendency most closely linked to the so-called culture of materials, descended from Tatlin and the Productivists, and through Vesnin that he pursued his attempt at a synthesis between geometric abstraction and material concreteness. The filigree of metallic structure and the aerial superstructures—which together constitute the formal repertory most preferred by Vesnin—were almost literally incorporated into Leonidov's compositions, where such elements are always recognizable even though they are brought together in a different manner and combined with volumetric surfaces—the latter being more essential, more clearly traceable to abstract-geometric principles of composition.

Such a synthesis became possible on the level of formal conventions, the level on which Leonidov permitted his students to operate "in order to learn how to think in architecture, even through abstract categories," and on which it was possible to attempt a precise recovery of the bi-dimensional geometry of Malevich, particularly with regard to hypotheses of planning which sought to project and extend a spatial-formal organization planimetrically into the landscape. (We should also remember Gan's call for a reassessment of Malevich's work at the time Gan was working for *SA* and was very close to Leonidov.)

Thus we arrive at an analysis of a more specifically historical nature. It now should be directed at historically situating the main typological features of Leonidov (the new man and the heir to the avant garde) in a defined context, namely the one with which Russian intellectuals were confronted following the dramatic transformation of Soviet history at the end of the 1920s.

Within this historical dimension, Leonidov's earlier distinguishing features—the novelty of his person, his continuity with respect to the avant garde—take on an entirely new meaning; distanced from the utopian formulations of the early 1920s, they become the hallmarks of a deathly premoni-

tion, a fatal condemnation of the new man as impotent, as the unprepared witness to an extraordinary structural upheaval.

Moreover, and it is this that matters most in a situation where actual history is the necessary condition for comparison, explanations now emerge for Leonidov's contradictions and internal tensions, especially for the presence, in his lucid thought, of crisscrossing tensions between the distant and opposite poles of past and future, poles sharing an essential characteristic that surely should not be ascribed to the present, that should not be contaminated by the contingencies and imperfections of reality.

On the one hand we have the prophetic foreshadowings of a future devoid of tensions, governed according to harmonic, hygienic (one might even say loyal and comradely) living relations, even in the workplace, in factories redeemed by environmental design and technology, in offices made completely healthy by their contact with nature, in houses transformed into veritable environments of physical culture and organized into small groups (according to new moral and aesthetic standards which made it possible to say, "life is beautiful!"). On the other hand we have the almost infantile, childlike discovery of the characteristics of Old Russia, of the vivid and scintillating chroma of the world of ancient images, the vast and available space in which are situated the objects propelled by fantasy. All these ancient testimonies were so distant and so different from the testimony of the present that they appeared as objects beyond time, outside of history. The search for a new language had to take place, it seems, outside of history, in order to assimilate from the past the elements of a repertory that was as vast as it was rich in images and rules.

In this light, the "laconism" of Leonidov's abstract geometry appears to be quite different from that of Mies, to whom he has often been compared. The latter's laconic manner is completely rooted in history. The idea of order in Mies is linked almost directly to German Romantic Classicism, to a sense of completeness and perfection inherent in the ascendancy of a bourgeoisie which is at once rationalistic and restorative. In Leonidov, on the other hand, the need for a formal order seems to derive precisely from the ahistorical situation of his

12 work, from the forward flight of his technological utopia together with his constant looking back to the mythic past of old Russia and its accumulated formal institutions. After all, does not the interest in philological excavation, from the rediscovery of the work to the uncovering of the very root of its primitive genesis, perhaps amount to the most authentic and profound aspect of the primordial Futurism of V. Klebnikov, the acknowledged father of the literary avant garde?

Surely Leonidov's declared predilections for Oriental art, his memory of the works he executed with the iconographic master of his native village and of the whole countryside of Vlasikha, his attentive study of monuments, beginning with St. Basil, or of the color in Rublev's paintings, must have left a profound impression on him, not only with regard to expressive techniques like those employed in his drawings on a black ground, the egg temperas animated by golds and silvers on wooden plates, but also with regard to the more generally syntactical aspects of his compositions of volumes and elements (the chromatism of matchings, the arrangements of volumetric units in a discrete, discontinuous manner, the subordination of secondary elements to an emergent and polarizing result, etc.). "Doesn't it look like St. Basil?" said Leonidov, commenting on the effect of great variety produced by the chance matching of several multicolored toys of Viatka.

The futurist optimism and the notion of a history outside of time constitute the most visible proof of a total absence, at this point, of any effective grasp of reality on the part of the avant garde at the end of the 1920s. The socialization of the means of production, the planning of "socialism in one single country," snapped the fine thread that had sustained the promise of an ideological convergence between the intellectuals and the political class in power, drawn together around the themes of propaganda and technical-scientific information in the exceptional years of the Revolution and the NEP.

It would be useless at this point to discuss contrary hypotheses that assert either a natural or a violent death of the avant garde. What is most evident is that a historical condition emerged in which the problematic relationship between intellectual and political classes constituted only a secondary aspect of a larger and more complex whole.

The flight forward no longer only concerned the sphere of intellectual interest and formal superstructures. Teleological economic planning now not only reduced any physical planning decisions to a subordinate role, but also defined the cultural horizon, now formidably monolithic, to which every intellectual endeavor had to conform. The collective goal was now the attainment of predetermined production and planning objective, aimed teleologically at a previously established target.

The formal search for symbolic qualities, their projection into the hypothetical future of the Soviet new man, took on more the flavor of a depth sounding—although according to a collateral directrix—than of an experimentation converging with the ideology of a political plan. It seems that behind the hermeticism of the abstract and geometric forms lay the desire to investigate the possibilities of a new cosmic spirituality extending beyond the actual dimensions of time and space—a spirituality thus totally foreign to a Marxist conception of history and nature, and unconnected to any moralistic *telos* of bourgeois origin. The fountain planned by Leonidov in 1937-1938 for the sanatorium at Kizlovodsk, with its precise, complex arrangement of volumes, colors, water jets, Aeolian sonorities, etc., seems to symbolize perfectly this tendency toward a purely formal hermeticism and perfection.

The unexpected "return to nature," which around 1930 had affected Ginzburg (and Tatlin as well, during the period when he was dedicated to research into human flight), now also interested several members of the OSA who succumbed to the fascination of the facile philosophical-economic theories of M. Okhitovich, whose "de-urbanist" theory also exerted a considerable influence on the work of Leonidov, particularly in his project for the socialist settlement of Magnitogorsk.

It is no accident that within the OSA itself and on the editorial staff of *SA* there developed a very lively polemic around these issues. A. Vesnin, author of several proposals for residential communes (*dom-kommuna*), did not agree with the anti-urban conception of the dispersive linear city as projected by Ginzburg, Okhitovich, Barshch, and Sokolov; and it can be

This essay was originally published in unabridged form in Ivan Leonidov, *Vieri Quilici and Massimo Scolari, editors.* Milan: Franco Angeli Editore, 1975.

equally assumed that he did not approve of Leonidov's unusual proposal for a "carpet" to be unrolled across the landscape, comprised of roads, greenery, public buildings (low structures of various shapes), prisms of tall residential blocks, and checkerboards of low-rise houses grouped around courtyards.

It is also no accident that, along with the controversy over the de-urbanist model, there developed a polemic about Leonidov's architecture with regard to his abstract, formalist language. Alexander Vesnin himself, and later N. Krasilnikov, Jolovkin, as well as younger figures such as A. Aleksandrov, Bogdanov, Kibriev, Kuzmin, and Zhirov, supported the rationale and the validity of Leonidov's formal research whom they all regarded as an "architect–innovator." And yet, it was precisely because of the bitter polemics surrounding these issues that the OSA entered into a crisis late in 1930.

As members of the avant garde became more detached from reality (above all from a general sense of usefulness), that is, not only removed from the illusory but still important function of propaganda but later definitely cut off from the concrete economic implementation of the political plan, they seemed to vacillate in an uncertain manner—as uncertain as the early manifestations of Socialist Realism—between continuing as individuals with laboratory research on the philological excavation of the work, on the one hand, and making a drastic, impossible attempt at compromise, at ideological synthesis, on the other.

In reality, after 1930 the Soviet intellectual found himself on the threshold of an aesthetic activity which was characterized not so much by an improbable desire on the part of political power to persecute avant-garde art as such but rather by a fundamental and painful uncertainty, an awareness of having unexpectedly reached a fatal state of relative uselessness. Only in this light can one understand the individual and collective metamorphosis of an entire generation to a commitment to an activity that today still seems to characterize the aesthetic experience in the Soviet Union. Since the 1930s, there seems to have come into being an aesthetics of suggestion, no longer nourished by faith in a practical intellectual

utopia, but tending instead to the broadening of cognitive data of an anthropological and humanistic nature.

In examining the cosmic images and the technological spaces extendable to the infinite, precarious parallels can be seen to exist between Leonidov and other aesthetic experience in the Soviet Union, even those of recent date. For instance, both a nostalgia for an uncontaminated Nature—almost as a regret for a lost state of existence—and a search for an anthropological and scientific totality are still today widespread themes in Soviet culture.

Although Leonidov indubitably belonged to the period of the avant garde, he had already begun to delineate, in substance, the essential features of a later aesthetic production which would give up representing the contents of a specific historical period, at least in any explicit way, preferring instead the indefinite dimension of a so-called socialist neo-Humanism.

Notes
1. See A. Kopp, *Ville et Révolution*, Paris, 1967, p.200. On the same subject see also "Leonidov morte del costrutivismo" in V. Quilici, *L'architettura del costruttivismo*, Bari, 1969, pp.167-177, and S. Khan Magomedov, "I.I. Leonidov, 1902-1960," in *Maratrè* n.14-15, 1965. Some of the more illustrious ideologues of the Revolution also devoted themselves to the theme of the Soviet *new man*, such as A. Lunacharsky for example. In "Il nuovo uomo russo" (in *La rivoluzione proletaria e la cultura borghese,* by A. Lunacharsky, 1923. Italian translation: Milan, 1972) Lunacharsky, while adopting a position clearly opposed to the "leftist" avant gardist intellectuals of the period (Lefism, Biomechanics, Constructivism which are defined by Lunacharsky as "our ideological catarrh"), nonetheless asserts the need for definitively overcoming "Oblomovism"—the Russian-peasant cultural model consisting of renunciation and dream—in addition to the need for "fortifying techno-practical culture" with a generation made up of "youth, as well as, in a considerable measure, of the most advanced part of the working class," and endowed with the revolutionary impetus needed for the "organization of every aspect of Soviet life." "The Young people, continues Lunacharsky, "ardently desire to become lucid, rational, *capable; they* want to mould themselves to the point of becoming hardened, scientifically trained and fit combatants fighting against the desolation that afflicts all of Russia, against the abandoned state of our forests and our boundless steppes. But this is not enough. This dereliction afflicts not only uncultivated areas but also all of our countryside with its still tremendous backwardness, (it afflicts) our cities and even

14 ourselves. We are still poorly organized. We, all of Russia, are as though waiting for a great organizing force which would not only mine our coal and our other minerals, not only electrify the whole country, but would find in ourselves the sources of energy which we don't know how to use, and would activate those contacts that permit a regular interaction between the liveliness of our thought and our work force." In this passage, as we can see, are present, above and beyond the anticonstructivist polemic, all the arguments characteristic of the ideology of the *new world,* arguments filtered through a faithful waiting for a (transcendental?) 'organizing force.'"

2. In this famous piece of writing one reads: "The struggle for a new vision of artistic labor started with the Constructivists in the RSFSR in 1920. The ideal content of Constructivism was concretized in abandoning the metaphysical substance of the aesthetic ideal and in following the path of a consequent artistic materialism. The Constructivists set themselves these problems: to liquidate the abstract forms and the old vision of art, and even more to rationalize artistic labor. This current brought together the masters of theatrical labor (Meyerhold, Tairov and others) and painters and poets of the left. *In this way was Constructivism denatured and vulgarized.* (...)" See "Nasa spravka" in *SA* n.2, 1926.

In 1927 ("Spravka o Kazimire Malevice," in *SA,* n.3, 1927.) A. Gan, on the other hand, asserted that "the novelty, the purity and the originality of Suprematist abstract compositions undoubtedly foster a new psychologico-perceptual attitude towards volumetrico-spatial masses. This will soon be recognized as one of Malevich's great merits. The eventual insertion of his practical works in the universities will teach our youth how to execute their academic works in a new way, even qualitatively speaking." Krinsky, who was involved after 1919 with Ladovsky in transferring to the field of planning the formal lessons originating in the figurative experiments of Malevich and Tatlin, also wrote, "The Suprematist compositions of Malevich, with their predominant employment of combinations of rectangles, were close to combinations of simplified, architectonic volumes projected into the sphere of representation (...) but more than anyone else it was Tatlin who aroused our interest." See "Architekturnaja mysl'nacala 20ch godov" by V. Khazanova in *Sovetskaya arkhitekt pervych let lktjabria,* Moscow, 1970, pp.11-42.

3. M. Ginzburg himself, in 1923 in *Ritm v architekture,* had emphasized the importance of the formal—autonomous—structure of the architectural work, "Architecture...on the one hand is the result of a set of material, functional, and technical conditions, and on the other it is the result of a world of autonomous, totally abstract forms (...) Direct analysis leads us to the belief that in all these complicated architectural monuments (...) the fundamental elements are formed by the combination of simple geometric bodies (...) The laws of rhythm define themselves as the essence of any architectural work." See V. Khazanova, *op.cit.*

Ivan Leonidov

S. Khan-Magomedov
Translated by Milka Bliznakov

Leonidov's Lenin Institute Project was published in Sovremennaya Arkhitektura *n.4/5, 1927.*

Ivan Leonidov is almost a legendary figure in the development of Soviet architecture. For architects of the twenties, he was an idol to be emulated, while during the thirties and forties his name became synonymous with formalism; our architectural press coining the term *leonidovshchina* (in Leonidov's manner) to indicate formalism and fantasy. By the end of World War II, Leonidov was virtually forgotten.

In Soviet as well as in international architecture, the twenties was marked by a search for new approaches to design methodology. The "new architecture" which had emerged during the previous decades now could be fully developed as a result of the Russian Revolution and the revolutionary spirit in a number of European countries.

In spite of fundamental social differences, there were many similarities in the 1920s between developments in Soviet architecture and the progressive movements in capitalist countries. These similarities were evident above all in the use of new materials and building techniques, in the incorporation of advances in applied science and construction, and the search for a new aesthetic of form.

In the West, this search was mainly in the sphere of the aesthetic rationalization of new asymmetrical structures, based on simple geometric volumes devoid of traditional decoration. To some extent these things were also characteristic of Soviet architecture, although here the formal–aesthetic research was permeated by a revolutionary romanticism and carried out in the name of producing new artistic imagery. This gave a definite advantage to Soviet architecture, for the formal–aesthetic issues in our country were bound up with the ideological–artistic ones. In spite of this, our architectural approach remained one-sided because it did not consider what was most important, namely changes in the functional purpose of buildings, and therefore this approach led to artificially symbolic compositions. This is especially true in the work of the Association of New Architects (ASNOVA), founded in 1923.

Within this polemical approach to contemporary architecture a method arose in the 1920s that was based on the correct solution to functional problems rather than on a preoc-

15

cupation with new methods and ways of design. Here Soviet Constructivism and West European functionalism played a decisive role in the development of the "new architecture." However, these movements in their orthodox form (Gropius, Ginzburg) were subject to certain limitations in their artistic expression largely as a result of their polemical antipathy to single-minded aesthetic research. In the main the functionalists concentrated on achieving correct plan forms for a wide range of building tasks, while the followers of ASNOVA paid more attention to the invention of new, unusual, and sometimes preconceived volumes.

Thus, during the 1920s Soviet and West European architecture came up with a host of unprecedented and interesting designs and approaches in terms of building technology, functionalist method, and formalist aesthetics. In due course the question of how one should synthesize all these achievements became critical, as did the issue of attaining a satisfactory spatial resolution in the context of contemporary architecture. These difficulties were solved neither by the functionalists nor by the aesthetic–formalists. For it proved to be necessary to go beyond plan organization and to consider the spatial ordering of functional processes.

To resolve these problems the architect had to be a thinker, a creator–inventor, and a superb artist. Among the more significant figures of the 1920s one must cite both Le Corbusier and Leonidov. Their works grew in part out of the combination of functionalist methodology with formalist experimentation and in part out of a conjunction of scientific technology with a new socio–architectural typology. By synthesizing in their works the achievements of the twenties, each from his own ideological position, they succeeded in arriving at a "resolution of space," and thus in forcibly influencing the development of the "new architecture."

Ivan Il'ich Leonidov was born in 1902 to a farmer–forester family, on Vlasikh farm in the Staritskii area, in the Tver' gubernatorial district which is today known as the Kalinin region. After completing the four-year village primary school, the twelve–year–old youth went to St. Petersburg, where for several years he worked as a temporary laborer in the dockyards while helping his family during the summer with the harvesting. From childhood Leonidov loved to draw, displaying a preference for portrait painting. After seeing his early drawings, an icon painter from Tver' accepted him as an apprentice. In 1919, Leonidov joined the newly organized Tver' art school, and in 1921 he was sent to continue his education at the Vkhutemas in Moscow, where he began by studying art, only to transfer later to the architectural teaching unit of the Vesnin brothers.

Leonidov's unusual talents were quite evident in his student years. His studio project for a swimming pool was immediately noticed by A. Vesnin. From his third year onward, he entered many architectural competitions and won several awards, including ones for a project for an improved peasant cottage (1925), for a prototypical workers' club for 500 to 1000 people (1926), and for a housing complex in Ivanovo-Voznesensk (1925).

Leonidov's destiny thereafter was unusual. His diploma project for the Lenin Institute and Library displayed in the first exhibition of contemporary architecture in Moscow in 1927, impressed everyone. In an article entitled "Summation and Perspective on SA," analyzing the development of Constructivism during the first decade of the Soviet regime, M. Ginzburg distinguished Leonidov's Lenin Institute proposal as one of the major milestones in Constructivist development.

As is well known, the rapid spread of Constructivist principles in Soviet architecture led to the acceptance of this approach by many architects, not only as a new professional method, but also as a fashionable style. There was an immediate risk of canonizing certain interpretations of Constructivism and turning these into the superficial elements of a formal order. In this respect, Leonidov's Lenin Institute project had a very special significance.

Ginzburg wrote of Leonidov's project, "Among all other exponents at the SA exhibition it stands out by virtue of its original apporach. Superbly rendered in a number of fine drawings and in a precise model, it clearly constitutes a courageous architectural–spatial solution. This work is of importance to us above all because it is a definite breakthrough; it goes beyond all schemes and elements which have become inevitable, habitual, and customary and which at best are the result of common method and at worst bring us dangerously close to the adoption of stylistic stencils. Though based in our common principles, Leonidov's Library pioneers a purely spatial, architectural solution which in its reorganization of the very idea of a town leads away from both traditional building form and the gridded urban space in which such a form may materialize."[1]

Encouraged by the success of his project, Leonidov designed a number of projects between 1927 and 1930 in rapid succession: a government building in Alma-Ata (1927-1928), the Centrosoyuz building in Moscow (1928), a series of Film Studios (1928), the Columbus Memorial (1929), a New Type of Social Club (1929), a House of Industry (1929-1930), a Palace of Culture on the site of the Simonov monastery (1930), and a number of alternative proposals, "projects for socialist population resettlement," in the new industrial complex of Magnitogorsk (1930).

These three years were the period of truly creative ascendancy for the young architect. He successfully expanded many ideas already expressed in general terms in the project for the Lenin Institute. Leonidov's authority, popularity, and international reputation grew with each year as his projects were published in foreign periodicals. He actively participated in the public life of our country, emerged as a leader of the Society of Contemporary Architects (OSA), and became a member of the editorial board of its publication, the journal *Contemporary Architecture*. He went on to deliver a paper at the first congress of OSA, and so forth.

One of the most important urban design problems in Soviet architecture was the problem of the social center. Although during the 1920s, the Constructivists as well as the functionalists paid particular attention to integrating communal services into large housing complexes, the problem of creating appropriate social centers for the housing schemes, i.e., of concentrating in one place the most necessary elements and systems for the maintenance of communal social life was virtually ignored.

In Western architecture, especially after the Second World War, shopping centers became principal organizing elements. Owing to capitalist conditions, commercial establishments proved to be the most viable parts in a network of social services, above all because they were income-producing. Meanwhile, structures for children, schools, clubs, or sports did not always materialize, even if they were supposed to be designed in conjunction with housing.

In Soviet architecture growing attention was already being paid during the 1920s to building types which emphasized new social aspects, such as the workers' clubs designed by the brothers Vesnin, Golosov, etc. while Leonidov also explored various types of club buildings, urban social and educational centers within housing neighborhoods.

This was already implicit in the project for the Lenin Institute. Leonidov considered it "a collective research center"; it comprised a library with a stack capacity of fifteen million volumes, five reading rooms for from 500 to 1000 people, an institute for library sciences, a research institute, an auditorium capable of accommodating a wide range of audiences (from 250 to 4000 people), and a planetarium (a theater for the sciences).

In 1929, Leonidov delivered a report to the First Congress of OSA on a new type of social club which in his opinion should become the center of cultural life for the entire population. Leonidov thought that the club should not only be a place for relaxation and entertainment, but also the virtual organizer of the social life of the population, the social center of any housing complex. Leonidov's report was illustrated by his proposal for such a club. Regarding the club as a social center which would be in daily use by the entire population, he calculated the size of the site for its accommodation and then transformed the available space into a unique cultural and recreational center which included a library with reading rooms, laboratories, rooms expressly designed for seminars, films, and meetings, a gymnasium, a winter garden with a swimming pool, an exhibition space, a multi-use space for sports activities and films, a children's pavilion with playroom and pool, certain areas of outside space for demonstrations (parade grounds), and a section allocated for outdoor sports and a park.

18 Leonidov developed this idea for a club complex further in his project for the Palace of Culture on the Simonov monastery site. "The Palace of Culture," he wrote, "organizes the neighborhood's entire system of political enlightenment and cultural education on the basis of mass amateur activity programs for the workers and according to the diverse development of the workers' own initiatives."[2]

The site of the Palace of Culture was divided into four sections: a physical development section (stadium, athletic fields, indoor swimming pool, gymnasium, etc.) with spaces for relaxation; a section for mass assemblies (a large auditorium with a transformable interior, a lobby, and a dining room); a section for historical sciences (a museum with lecture rooms); and fields for mass demonstrations.

In the circumstances of those years and indeed even today, it was patently unrealistic to create such a large complex for each housing neighborhood, especially in the dense urban fabric of Moscow. Nevertheless, this project is of interest for its daring attempt to create a socio-cultural complex with appropriate provisions for the town of the future. These ideas were later utilized in Russia for the creation of urban and regional parks dedicated to culture and recreation, where similar principles of functional zoning, of subdivision into sections for sports and for relaxation, and so forth were widely applied.

A new understanding of the planning and building of the contemporary town and of its spatial organization had already appeared with the Lenin Institute project. Leonidov located his scientific-social complex on the Lenin Hills in a hypothetical "new town," freely laid out on the large site. He conceived of the contemporary urban architectural ensemble not as a piece of "organized" space "cut out" from the densely built town, but rather as an ensemble of structures, as a composition "holding together" a definite part of the surrounding space; that is to say, not as buildings, but rather as buildings projected into space. Space played a unifying, not a subordinate role. Leonidov developed this method further in other projects (the Columbus Memorial, the Film Studios, etc.). A similar principal of free spatial composition was applied after the war in the planning of the administrative center for the new capital of Brasilia. Examined separately, the projects for the Lenin Institute and the Simonov monastery club complex might give the impression that Leonidov was in agreement with the de-urbanists' views during the 1920s because he provided large, freely built areas for his structures, but this is not the case. One needs to bear in mind the role that Leonidov assigned to such complexes within urban life. He perceived them not as pompous assemblies but as centers for the neighborhood's daily social life.

A tradition was established in Soviet architecture during the subsequent period (1930-1960) to create such centers out of administrative facilities and buildings dedicated to spectacles, while clubs and recreation facilities began to acquire the character of commercial establishments. They often lost any authentic social character because of their external pomposity and their ostentatious "made for the masses" facades. Today, under the influence of foreign development, we often make the shopping center the core of the housing neighborhood, and this is hardly correct.

In my opinion, despite certain shortcomings and mistakes, Soviet architecture in the 1920s correctly formulated the principles of authentic social building types, those where man does not enter merely as a consumer or a visitor to an administrative facility, or as a sports spectator, but rather as a direct participant in social life. Leonidov's club complexes were free of redundant pomposity and any commercial facilities, but they were nonetheless centers for the neighborhood's social life.

Leonidov's urban design ideas were aspirations, looking to the future, combining everything valuable from the theories of both the urbanists and the de-urbanists. All this is exemplified by his approach to resolving the problem of the housing neighborhood. By the time of his project for the Palace of Culture on the site of the Simonov monastery, Leonidov had initiated a "scheme for population resettlement and the organization of cultural life." But the idea of the organization of an entire housing neighborhood was only to be developed in detail in his "project for socialist resettlement" at the Magnitogorsk chemical-metallurgical plant.

In this project Leonidov rejected the usual repetitive rows of housing blocks; nor did he use the de-urbanists' models of low-rise housing or house-communes connected to public spaces by enclosed walkways which were fashionable at the time. In 1930 he employed mixed–use planning for the housing neighborhood, an approach which has only been widely adopted during the last few years. However, unlike contemporary mixed–use planning, which usually consists of tower–like high–rises with elevators, three–to–five–storey housing without elevators, and other low–rise houses, Leonidov utilized only two types of housing—high–and low–rise. Evidently, he understood even then that economic factors and principles of convenience would eliminate the need for medium–height housing without elevators in the future.

The Magnitogorsk project assumed the linear form of alternating housing blocks (two high–rise towers and eight low–rise units) with interspersed sections for children (nurseries, kindergartens, play areas, swimming pool). Adjoining the housing clusters were sections to be given over to clubs and to social and reacreational facilities. The public transportation arteries connecting the housing to the industrial plants were isolated from the housing neighborhoods, and pedestrian overpasses served to connect the housing zones to the recreational complexes.

Contrary to the principle of creating a green area with facilities for children, sports, and rest in the center of the neighborhood, Leonidov advanced the principle of opening the entire housing complex to nature. He proposed to locate the public buildings at the periphery of the complex, modulating gradually from the high–rise towers to the low–rise public buildings and then to the recreational facilities, parks, and gardens. A similar principle of structuring the housing complex was put into practice later in some of the satellite towns built in the Scandinavian countries.

In a note attached to this project, Leonidov wrote, "The socialist population resettlement is not the old town of elementary blocks scooped out from nature and accidentally connected to industry, which deprives man of the pulse of life through its monotony." Leonidov aspired to create "housing surrounded by gardens, recreation areas, and swimming pools, thus precluding the need for vacation developments outside of the towns. A form of dwelling where labor, rest, and culture are organically bonded together."[3]

For Leonidov, the years 1927-1930 were a period of search, reflection, and creative formation. Leonidov considered every one of his projects as arising from the need to create a new socialist and communist way of life. It is a characteristic of his work that it attempted to unify the social meaning of design with a mastery of artistic form. However, since this field was still in the process of growth, Leonidov's projects were not free from abstract social eccentricities, as were the works of many other architects during this period. In spite of this, many of his proposals are still of considerable interest today with regard to the social significance of architecture.

During his student years, Leonidov had followed a functional method of determining the volumetric–spatial composition of a building. Accordingly, he would subdivide the interior into separate elements, depending on their function, and then interconnect them according to the consecutive sequence of the given technological process, such as in his project for a printing plant or in his clubs for 500 and 1000 people, among others. Later, Leonidov followed the procedure of unifying the interior space and reinforcing its connection with nature while siumltaneously simplifying the volumetric–spatial composition of the building itself.

Of interest in this respect is the interior organization of a typical housing unit in the Magnitogorsk project. At the center is a high foyer space which extends openly in four directions and connects to sixteen small, one-room living units without any intermediate corridors. This central space was intended to serve as a dining room, as a place for morning exercises, and as a common space for relaxation. In principle Leonidov was against corridors and connecting elements. He loved large, open interior volumes directly related to nature through curtain-wall fenestration and containing within both planting and water. At the same time, he understood the necessity of separating the dwelling from the work place. As in his typical dwelling, Leonidov totally eliminated corridors in his project for the House of Industry.

He aimed at creating new working conditions for the employees. Each group of employees according to its specialization would occupy a typical floor, each floor housing about 120 people.

Here is what he wrote in the explanatory note attached to this project: "each floor space is subdivided according to the number of people, with separate spatial allocations of five square meters per person, excluding walkways. There are no dividing partitions. Between these areas are planters with greenery; the floor and ceiling are of soft, noise-absorbing material. On one side of these areas is a zone for relaxation and recreation exercises, structured by sofas for relaxation; there is also a library, spaces for meals served from below, showers, a swimming pool, walking and running tracks, and spaces for receiving guests."[4]

In the ground floor of the single-story wing there was to have been a meeting room, a sports hall, club rooms, cloakrooms, etc., and on the roof of this wing were a movable swimming pool, athletic areas, and a running track. The top floor consisted of a hotel for newcomers, with an open restaurant in the center and a space for strolling in the open air. The stairway and elevators were grouped together in a separate volume adjacent to the main building. Moreover, the restaurant, hotel, and roof (places for relaxation and recreation) could be reached by a separate elevator.

In remarking on Leonidov's approach to the internal organization of the buildings of his day, one needs to note such innovations as the invention of the transformable multi-purpose auditorium as in the Lenin Institute project. This auditorium-*cum*-planetarium, circular in plan, could be subdivided by movable partitions into segments; each segment having different seating capacities. Part of the auditorium could also be made to serve as a tribune during mass demonstrations by extending its form out into nature through the removal of wall panels.

In his Palace of Culture, Leonidov included a circular "hall for demonstrations" with a wide-span, hemispherical roof. This hall also could be subdivided into separate sections, while the seats could be moved around the circle or stacked underneath the floor to provide clear space. The principles involved in resolving the volumetric-spatial composition of each of these individual buildings as worked out by Leonidov were to be of great import in the future development of the world's architecture. Leonidov did not aim at uniting spaces with different purposes into one complicated organism in order to create "expressive" dynamic compositions. He correctly sensed that a fundamental tendency in the shaping of modern architecture would be the desire for simple volumes. In the Lenin Institute he boldly designed the tall building in the form of an all-glass rectangular prism and the auditorium in the shape of a sphere. Thereafter, in projects for housing and office buildings, he employed simple exterior volumes in the shape of tall glass prisms, either square or rectangular in plan. This was a novelty in the 1920s. Modern architecture spontaneously evolved toward such simple volumes, which were to receive wide acceptance only much later, for the most part after the war. Mies van der Rohe is usually regarded as the originator of the "simplicity." However this is not strictly true, since by the late 1920s Leonidov had already worked out all the basic methods propagated today as the methods of "the school of Mies van der Rohe."

Leonidov was the first to propose a housing high-rise in the form of a glass prism (Magnitogorsk). Mies realized such housing towers in Chicago only in 1951. Leonidov was the first to create a project for an office building in the form of a soaring glass prism with the first floor extending our underneath—the House of Industry. Bunshaft's famous "Lever House" in New York which follows the same compositional principles was built only in 1950. The horizontal organization of interchanging glass and slab—as in the Centrosoyuz project—was also advanced by Leonidov long before such buildings were constructed in the West.[5]

It must be stressed that almost all buildings designed by Leonidov during the 1927-1930 period were simple volumes with maximum glazing. In all these projects, Leonidov demonstrated that simple geometric volumes without any decoration could be considerably more expressive than complex organizations and groupings of such volumes. The bold use of extremely simple volumes (prism, cylinder, hemisphere, pyramid, etc.) was truly innovative during the

1920s, a time when architects were searching for the expressive potentialities of the "new architecture" by bringing together a variety of geometric forms and striving to compensate for the lack of decoration by complicating the volumetric and spatial composition of the building.

Along with all of these achievements, one should also note that in his daring, ingenious search Leonidov frequently was carried away by the purely formal aspects of his beloved pyramidical and hemispherical glass volumes, employing them alike for spaces with diverse purposes, regardless of their functional suitability and technical limitations. He no doubt also overused such elements as radio antennas, dirigible docking masts, etc.

The crucial point, however, is that Leonidov's creative designs did not arise from his desire to invent new symbolic forms as was typical of K. Melnikov, for example), but from his utilization of the achievements of contemporary technology, exploiting to the utmost the potential of the new techniques. This is partially evident in the project for the Lenin Institute, where all the structural elements were calculated by the engineer, A. Urmaev, in accordance with the technical possibilities of the time.

Nonetheless, it should be noted that a number of Leonidov's projects were marked by a degree of utopianism. However, even this seemingly most weak aspect in his work can largely be explained by the euphoric circumstances of the 1920s, and particularly by Leonidov's distinct talent and disposition for experimental design. Given that experimental design always has the right to take place, and bearing in mind that the twenties was a period in which one strived to establish the new social meaning of socialist architecture, it is not surprising that experimentation became the norm in architectural design.

During the 1920s, experimental design was a kind of creative laboratory wherein the most crucial problem was to define the direction that such experiments should take. An analysis of the design competitions from this period demonstrates that many of the architects, infatuated with "paper architecture," lost touch not only with the reality of the pre-sent, but also with any understanding of future probabilities. Still, Leonidov's works from the end of the 1920s to the beginning of the 1930s can hardly be explained in these terms, even if his "architectural fantasies" were "utopian" to the extent that none of his projects of these years were built. Nonetheless, Leonidov's impetuous creative growth during the 1927-1930 period sustained the hope that a great master had arrived in Soviet architecture. At the age of twenty–eight, he became one of the leading architects, not only in the Soviet Union, but also world wide.

Yet, just when he was at the threshhold in the 1920s and 1930s, Leonidov's destiny was overtaken by a severe test which had a negative impact on his future creative work. This period was characterized by the rise and activity of certain organizations in various art fields which proclaimed a polemical exclusivity. These organizations inflicted substantial damage on the development of Soviet art by vulgarizing Marxist–Leninist teachings about the role of the arts in society; under the guise of fighting for a "proletarian art" they indulged in ferocious, confrontational criticism. These critical campaigns also affected architecture. Their effect was manifested primarily in the persecution of all those engaged in independent creative thought. It is hardly accidental that the first victim of this criticism was an architect whose work most clearly expressed his disposition toward innovation. At the end of 1930, when Leonidov had just completed the Palace of Culture on the former Simonov monastery site, ASI (Architecture–Structural Institute) organized a debate on "Leonidov's manner," during which Leonidov's works were subjected to sharp attack; thereafter, an article appeared in the periodical *Iskusstvo-v-massy (Art–in the Masses)* in which he was openly accused of working to the detriment of society.

In response to the unfair criticism of Leonidov's work, the magazine *Sovremennaya Arkhitektura* n.5, of 1930, published an article "Ot Redaktsii" ("From the editors"), reevaluating the uproar created by Leonidov's name.

"The editors of *SA*," the article states, "are aware of the faults found in some of I. Leonidov's projects: *deficiencies in realistic conditions, disregard for present economic feasibil-*

22 *ities, flirting with elements of aestheticism.* All these are undisputed deficiencies of Leonidov's works. Yet the critics of Leonidov's works do not see at all what, in our view, are enormous advantages and make Leonidov's work *far superior and more valuable in definite respects that the works of his rivals* despite all the deficiencies indicated above. The fact is that Leonidov advances in his projected work as an *architect–statesman* or *architect–thinker,* who does not blindly execute the building program but instead corrects it, sometimes reconstituting it, thus contributing everything that, in his viewpoint, would aid in the speedy reconstruction of a way of life based on fundamental socialist principles. Naturally, errors are inevitably unavoidable, as also are 'twists,' *I. Leonidov often errs, often 'twists.'* However, these errors *against which no one is insured* in no way should serve as an excuse for subjecting Leonidov to an unheard-of persecution only because he thinks about architecture in a personal way and a new way."[6]

However, the criticism spread by the press certainly affected Leonidov's creative work. During the next three years he designed a number of interesting projects but could not bring them to conclusion. Working In Giprogor during 1931, Leonidov went to the construction site of the new town Igarka for half a year; in a number of the projects he designed there, he laid the foundations for progressive ideas about planning and building under permafrost conditions, ideas which are only being developed now. Thereafter, he designed a club for the *Pravda* organization and worked on a project for Meyerhold's theater, and carried out a number of other works.

In 1933 Leonidov created one of his best works—the competition project for the Dom Narkomtiazhprom in the Red Square. The competition took place during a period of infatuation with ostentatious gigantism. Yet Leonidov remained true to himself again. He did not pursue complicated volumetric–spatial structures, but decided to create a complex of three independent, lofty towers interconnected by skywalk bridges. The three high–rises are clearly differentiated in form. The main structure, a rectangle in plan, develops his concept of the contemporary office building type; it precedes the appearance of similar structures abroad by many years. Leonidov designed his office tower as a vertical rectangle; the structural system is clearly exposed at the ground floor, while above the walls are treated as light, hanging glass screens. The second tower—round in plan and with plastic silhouette—has outside partitions made entirely of glass block. At night the inside lighting would have made it glow like a fairy–tale column.

Leonidov determined that the Narkomtiazhprom building had to be the dominant compositional component of Moscow's center. The project came to life, to a great extent, through his honest formalistic search. His intention to erect such a high structure as a complement to the magnificent ensemble from the past is still of great interest. The bold juxtaposition of the three high towers, different in the form and character of their exterior treatment, unifies the new technical achievements with an authentically creative evolution related to our tradition. The general composition of the Dom Narkomtiazhprom is also related to the structural principles of the St. Basil's church. It is as though Leonidov was repeating the composition of this monument at a new scale, in new materials, given to new social usage, thereby endowing the composition around the Red Square with a new unity—not by artificial styling, but through preserving its historically established architectural image.

It is also important that Leonidov did not remain captive to the simple geometric forms (circle, rectangle, square) typical of early Constructivism (and formalism), but that in his project for the Narkomtiazhprom he foresaw that simplicity of form could also be achieved by the employment of second-degree curves—as in the silhouette of the round tower and in the hyperbolic–parabaloid roof of the free-standing assembly hall. Such curves have been widely propagated abroad in the last ten to fifteen years, particularly in opposition to the simple geometry of functionalism. In Leonidov's works, however, we already see a natural transition toward them at the beginning of the 1930s, at a time when they were used only in the strictly engineering works of Freyssinet, Maillart, and others.

All this is important because ultimately Mies van der Rohe came very close to monotony by canonizing in his works the

This is an abridged version of an article first published in Sovetskaya Arkhitectura, *n.16, 1964.*

simple form of the rectangular prism. Leonidov, however, who employed extremely simple forms initially, as early as the second half of the 1920s, did not limit himself to rectangular volumes. He introduced the dome, the vault, and the cylinder and then proceeded to complex curves.

During the following years Leonidov designed a printing plant for *Izvestia* in Moscow, the interiors of the Palace of Pioneers in Moscow, the project for the sanitorium Chaigruziia, and others.

His work in the field of urban design is of the greatest interest: for example, the competition project for the reconstruction of Moscow proposing to expand the town in a southwest direction; the project for the settlement of Kliuchki in the Urals, where the idea of a socialist population resettlement was further developed; and the planning of Crimea's southern seashore (the development of the entire coast and the project for the Pioneer's camp "Artek" carried out in collaboration with others).

Of the few small but actually executed works of Leonidov, mention should be made of the stariway outside the sanitorium Ordzhonikidze in Kislovodsk (1937), which connects the park with the high plateau on which the sanitorium is located.

Leonidov was a remarkable master, a man with the hypersensitive soul of a dreamer and the head of a thinker. He was endowed with a creative fantasy and the ability to look far into the future. Now, when we restore the good name of people unjustly slandered in the past, we must also keep in mind that there were those whose creativity was damaged, talented people for whom the atmosphere created during the "cult of personality" era was pernicious.

Besides all this, Leonidov was one of the Soviet architects whose work played a significant role in the development of Soviet architecture. His innovative projects, well known abroad, already correctly formulated thirty years ago the problems of the spatial organization of the urban ensemble, the contemporary interior, and the exterior shape of built form. The central ensemble at the New York World's Fair of 1939 with its Trylon (three pylons) and Perisphere, and even

such ultra-modern structures as the United Nations in New York, all rose from the roots of Leonidov's Lenin Institute, his House of Industry, and his Narkomtiazhprom.

Leonidov's projects are surprisingly contemporary. Many of them, even if executed today, would look very modern. Now, at a time when everthing new and original can be successfully developed and actually constructed, we are turning with great interest to the period when the foundations of our architectural development were established. This period, unjustly declared in the past to be a period of continuous error, must be objectively studied in depth. It is by now clear that the correct foundations for Soviet architecture were by and large laid out during the 1920s. In this, the works of Ivan Leonidov played a most significant role.

Notes
1. M. Ya. Ginzburg, "Summary and perspectives of *SA*," *Sovremennaya Arkhitectura*, n.4-5, 1927, p.116.
2. *Sovremennaya Arkhitecktura*, n.5, 1930, p.5.
3. Sovremennaya Arkhitecktura, n.3, 1930, p.1.
4. Sovremennaya Arkhitektura, n.4, 1930, pp.1-2.
5. Magomedov exaggerates these claims of precedence, for what is at stake here is not precedence but the fact that both Leonidov and Mies van der Rohe were influenced by the same sensibility, namely, by Malevich's Suprematism. (Editor's note.)
6. At the time the editorial board consisted of M. Barshch, G. Vegman, the brothers Vesnin, V. Vladimirov, M. Ginsburg, I. Nikolaev, G. Orlov, A. Pastermak, R. Khiger, and others.

Propaganda poster. Moscow, c. 1929. (Center text) "Project for a new type of social club." (Top left) "...relying most of all on the consciousness of the leading strata of workers (male and female) the trade union must maintain an active system of work to develop elements of the new being." (Upper left) "What should not be shown and built." (Lower left) "What should not be built." (Upper right) "Nature with a palette and a dirigible." (Bottom right) "In place of theater."

...Опираясь на наиболее сознательные, передовые слои рабочих и работниц ⟍ профсоюзы должны вести активную систематическую работу по развитию элементов **НОВОГО БЫТА**

9

что **НЕ** надо показывать и строить

2

как **НЕ** надо строить

3

И. И. ЛЕОНИДОВ. ПРОЕКТ КЛУБА НОВОГО СОЦИАЛЬНОГО ТИПА
I. LEONIDOFF. NEUE SOCIALE FORM DES ARBEITERKLUBS

НА ЗЕМЛЮ

ПРИРОДА С ПАЛИТРЫ И ДИРИЖАБЛЯ

14

ВМЕСТО ТЕАТРА

Propaganda poster. Moscow, c. 1929. (Center text) "Man in the service of technology and Technology in the Service of Man." *(Top right)* "Spatial scheme of a cult organization." *(Bottom right)* "Screen depicting radio transmission." *(Lower bottom)* Gosorgany *(government organizations) should strengthen their assistance to cultural enlightenment work or trade unions with the aim of wider service to the members of the trade unions and their families. On the part of the Gosorgany it is necessary at first to step up club construction, allotments to local and landed participants of the club, physical culture building and so on."*

ЧЕЛОВЕК НА СЛУЖБЕ У ТЕХНИКИ И ТЕХНИКА НА СЛУЖБЕ У ЧЕЛОВЕКА

11

22

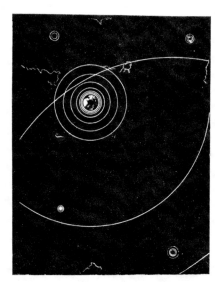

СХЕМА ПРОСТРАНСТВЕННОЙ КУЛЬТОРГАНИЗАЦИИ

ЭКРАН
ПРИНИМАЮЩИЙ ПЕРЕДАЧУ ИЗОБРАЖЕНИЯ ПО РАДИО

ГОСОРГАНЫ должны усилить свою помощь культурно-просветительной работе профсоюзов в целях более широкого обслуживания членов профсоюзов и их семей.
Со стороны госорганов необходимо в первую очередь обеспечить кредитование клубного строительства, предоставление помещений и земельных участков под клубы и физкультурные сооружения и т. п.

26 **Association of Architects of the Academy of Fine Arts, 1917:** This association, a sub-section of the official cultural organization of the state, was the first to be inaugurated after the February Revolution. Its members included A. Lunacharsky, A. Benoit, M. Gorky, Glazunov, and Malevich.

Moscow Association of Architects (MAO), 1918: Formed out of the Association of Architects when the Soviet government moved to Moscow, this organization had both practical and ideological aims. It devoted itself to the re-organization of education, building legislation, preservation, and the formation of social goals for architecture. In 1922, MAO began to organize architectural competitions and was involved in planning workers' housing, garden cities, clubs, banks, post offices.

Leningrad Association of Architects (LAO) and Association of Architects and Painters (OAKh), 1922: These two associations, preoccupied with the relationship of art to architecture, largely paralleled the activities of MAO, in Leningrad. They addressed themselves to factory buildings, housing estates, competitions, and the organization of training courses. In addition to this, they published a journal, *The Architect* (1924). A strong ideological dispute divided the Leningrad and Moscow associations, Leningrad regarding MAO as being overly involved with Western concepts.

New Association of Architects (ASNOVA), 1923: ASNOVA was founded by the leading professor at the Vkhutemas, N.A. Ladovsky and by his followers, Dokuchaev and Krinsky. This organization was dedicated to a strong alliance of architecture, painting, and sculpture and advocated the production of a collective cultural work force in collaboration with society. It attempted to establish a totally unprecedented approach to the creation of a formalist/structuralist architecture. At a certain point ASNOVA was closely affiliated with El Lissitzky and Melnikov.

Association of Urban Architects (ARU), 1928: Founded by Ladovsky and several other members who left ASNOVA, which they felt had become too involved with abstract theory, this group focussed on practical methods for reconstruction and land nationalization. ARU viewed architecture as a propaganda tool, and placed a strong emphasis on urbanism.

Association of Contemporary Architects (OSA), 1925: Founded by Moisei Ginzburg and the Vesnin brothers, this organization also included the LEF group (Leftist Art Front). In 1926 this group began to publish the magazine *Contemporary Architecture*. As the leading functionalist faction, OSA advocated a synthetic and modern technological approach and criticized ASNOVA for its lack of practical socialist ideas.

All-Russia Association of Proletarian Architects (VOPRA), 1929: In spite of its general popularity, OSA was criticized by VOPRA. This organization, involved in the planning of socialist estates and urban organization of Moscow, accused OSA of proliferating "bourgeois art" and utopic ideas. VOPRA rejected OSA's strident advocacy of technology and its denial of art. VOPRA held that architecture had to be proletarian both in its form and content; it had to be a synthesis of social, economic, emotional, and structural elements. The rivalry between VOPRA and OSA blinded them to the fact that many of their aims were similar.

Scientific All-Union Association of Architecture (VANO), 1930: VANO was in effect the coordinating organization of OSA, with branches throughout the country. It attempted to serve the Five-Year Plan in the areas of communal housing and the synthesis of industry with agriculture. VANO attempted to unite Marxist-Leninist theory with a sociology of architecture and art. It eventually absorbed ASNOVA, ARU, and OSA. OSA eventually became SASS (Sector of Architects for Socialist Construction) and worked closely with VANO in studying industrial settlements, working conditions, communal housing, transportation, and the design of provincial urban conditions.

In May, 1932, all architectural associations were incorporated under the Union of Soviet Architects of the USSR.

Interview with Ivan Leonidov

Q. How many of these clubs could the unions build right now?

A. Considering the urgency and the material possibilities, a single large one, perhaps a few smaller ones as well, maybe two...

Q. What are the capacity and costs of this club?

A. The capacity is about 2500 people. The costs, I do not underestimate them, about 500-600 rubles.

Q. Will the workers relax in your clubs?

A. The workers will relax in the club, in the health resort, in the rest home and in their own houses. There will be no absolute rest or relaxation. One gets tired by not working! One recovers from one type of effort through work of a different kind (for instance, by getting involved in intellectual work after physical labor). Only through a knowledge of this process is it possible to organize working hours, cultural development, and relaxation.

Q. When will the economic and technological conditions allow for the construction of such clubs?

A. Today only sceptics, reactionaries and hard-core defenders-of-tradition can ignore the scientific and technological means which are at our disposal right now! They do not understand that by using this potential, one can organize any cultural activity. Not looking beyond the tips of their noses, these people suggest having a cultural revolution the "old way;" they propose a "simple" industrialization—like tilling the ground with a hand-plow instead of a tractor. They abuse art, and titilate the masses with the mere pathos of industrialization. Only these people pretend that our present proposals for cultural organization are unreal fantasies.

Q. Are you aware of the effect of light on the human organism? What about the use of your glass walls in Baku, where people would be burned alive by the sun?

A. Climatic conditions have to be reflected in the construction of a wall; it is impossible simply to transplant to Baku what is intended for Moscow.

Q. Can you explain your method of putting different activities in identical forms—if it is not for purely formal aesthetic reasons?

A. This question shows that my interlocutor is mainly interested in appearances, in matters of taste, and not in concepts. Such an attitude is typical of those who are interested in idealistic architecture "as art." But to us, form is the product of a concept, of the functional interaction of workers and constructive moments. One should not criticize forms, but rather the method of cultural organization.

Q. Are you describing design or literature?

A. It depends on how you perceive it; to some people, Soviet power is not power, but a novella.

Q. Is one allowed to sing (in groups) in your club?

A. Please go ahead, if you derive some satisfaction from it. Yet, I believe that one should organize leisure activities inside the club in such a way that, by constantly raising the level of awareness, choral energy could be channelled into culturally significant activities.

Q. What should one hear on the radio, apart from music?

A. Life!

Q. Do you take into account the effect of colors on man's psyche?

A. There is no doubt that color affects man's psyche; the problem is how to switch from intuitive play with colors to intelligent research.

Q. How do you conceive of the organization of human emotions?

A. Emotions, abstract feelings cannot be analyzed scientifically—organizing emotions and feelings is essentially the organization of one's consciousness.

Q. Do you think it is essential to control visual impressions?

A. The problem is not to organize visual stimuli, but one's consciousness. The eye is a precise mechanism which transmits impressions to the brain. The negative or positive effect of visual stimuli depends on the social and class experiences of one's individual consciousness.

Q. Do you deny the significance of the theater and documentary film for the New Culture?

A. I deny the positive purpose of the theater, which has outlived its cultural role because of its primitive methods and techniques. Of course I do not deny film (documentary) as a technique for artists, but it is essential to organize it according to the Constructivist Method. Useless products such as Dziga Vertov's "Man with a Movie Camera" only undermine documentary film through their socially irresponsible way of showing life.

(Published in *SA*, n.3, 1929.)

Workers' Club for 500 and 1000 People

Moscow 1926

28   The Workers' Clubs were projected by Leonidov while he was a student at the *Vkhutemas*. The Workers' Club was a new type of building associated with particular factories in order to provide workers with leisure and educational facilities. A typical program consisted of a large auditorium for films, theater, political meetings, a cafeteria, a library, classrooms, a gymnasium, and hobby equipment.

In Leonidov's design for the club with a capacity for 500 people, the auditorium and lobby dominated the other facilities which were arranged in a long, two-storey block culminating in the gymnasium.

The club for 1000 people had a second lecture theater, and two garden "pits" for outside discussion and conversation.

1 Workers' club for 500 people. Moscow, 1926. Ivan Leonidov. Facade.
2 Workers' club for 500 people. Plan.
3 Workers' club for 1000 people. Ground floor plan and perspective.
4 Workers' club for 1000 people. First floor plan.

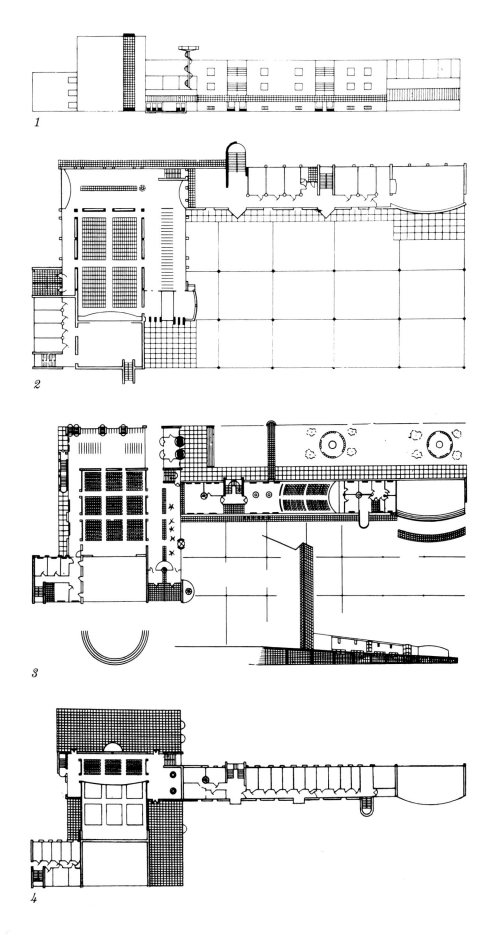

1

2

3

4

A Printing House for *Izvestia*

Moscow 1926

30   Leonidov designed the Izvestia Headquarters and Printing Works while he was still a student of Alexander Vesnin in the *Vkhutemas*. The project was composed of two buildings—a vertical tower and a horizontal slab—similar in plan and elevation. The vertical tower contained the editorial offices, while the horizontal building contained the printing works. The two structures connected to each other through a reception/information lobby.

Both buildings amounted to assemblies of transparent blocks suspended within external steel skeletons. The vertical tower acted as a totem-pole with a communication system running continuously along one side. This system fed the electric billboard at the top of the tower, providing an immediate presentation of the news generated inside the offices.

The lines of cubic vehicles, waiting alongside the presses to distribute the printed products, were considered as a mobile part of the composition. The facade, treated as an artistic organization of transparent and opaque surfaces, was devoid of any functional meaning.

The entire news complex would connect with the rest of the world through the freestanding radio mast behind the entrance lobby.

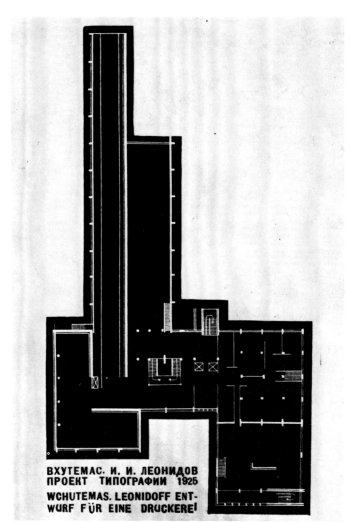

ВХУТЕМАС. И. И. ЛЕОНИДОВ
ПРОЕКТ ТИПОГРАФИИ 1925
WCHUTEMAS. LEONIDOFF ENT-
WURF FÜR EINE DRUCKEREI

1

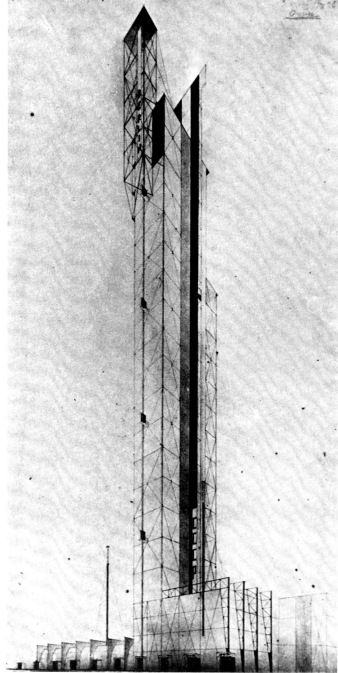

2

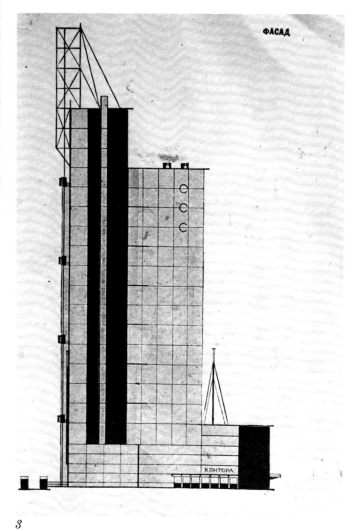

ФАСАД

КОНТОРА

3

1 Izvestia Printing House. Moscow,
1926. Ivan Leonidov.
Plan for printing office, designed at
Vkhutemas.
2 Izvestia Printing House. Perspective of tower.
3 Izvestia Printing House. Front
facade elevation.

Lenin Institute

Moscow 1927

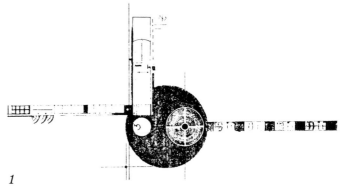

1

32 The Lenin Institute project, or as it was initially described, "the collective scientific center of the USSR," was a monument to the supremacy of science in the Marxist mythology. This final year design, executed in the *Vkhutemas,* was intended as a monument to the accessibility of scientific knowledge to every citizen. Its conception was an open invitation to participate in its projection.

As Magomedov writes (in *Building in the USSR* pp.124-125): "This (project) consisted of two principal forms; a vast auditorium—something of an innovation in itself—in the form of a sphere, glazed on the top half with seating in the lower half, and adjacent to it, the library, designed as a slender vertical element. The relationship of the two is a most important feature of the composition and this spatial dynamism was extended over the whole site in the arrangement of subordinate elements along three definite axes. This way of making more vital and unifying subsidiary spaces by the use of interlocking axes was exploited more than once by Leonidov. The real impact of his design derives from the extraordinary simplicity of his main forms—particularly striking since most other architects were seeking expression in complexity. In addition, he used the latest structural techniques in a most direct and dramatic way. His project was much approved at *Vkhutemas.*"

For his own part, Leonidov wrote the following description of this project in SA (n.4/5, 1927):
"*Intention*
To fulfil the needs of contemporary life by exploiting the ultimate possibilities of technology.
Theme
The Lenin Institute is the collective scientific center of the USSR.
Location
As part of a new city on the Lenin Hills, Moscow.
Elements
A library of fifteen million volumes, five reading rooms with capacities for 500 to 1000 people, and an Institute for Library Sciences. Auditorium with capacities for 250 to 4000 people, a science theater (planetarium), research institutes for separate scientific disciplines.

Mechanization
Library: delivery of books to and from the reader through a system of vertical and horizontal conveyor belts; upon request from the catalogue hall, the books are automatically delivered to the reading rooms.
Auditoria: mobile suspended walls can subdivide the sphere into the required number and type of auditoria. The entire glove can seat 4000; smaller crowds are accommodated in appropriate areas.
Planetarium: the sphere is converted into a science theater after the installation of projection screens on the inside skin. The globe also acts as a grandstand for mass meetings when it splits into two parts vertically, and the seats and walls of one hemisphere are rotated behind the other. Access to the auditorium is through a system of escalators from inside the podium below.
Research Institute: these institutes are connected to the auditoria and reading rooms by a number of installations: telephone, radio, etc. Organized in this way, the complete scientific collective of the Institute can be involved in a single project while physically located in different areas. An aerotram connects the Institute with the central aerotram station in Moscow."

Located high on a plateau atop the Lenin Hills (which define the basin of the Moscow Valley) the pure, reflective volumes of the Lenin Institute would be the dominating form on Moscow's horizon.

In an early version, two enormous balloons marked the location of the Institute from afar. A shuttle service aerotram (a silver capsule propelled by an aircraft engine suspended from a cable, tracing a diagonal trajectory from the top of the hills over the river, right into the heart of Moscow) emphasized the importance of the Institute. In this early version, the aerotram would land on the roof of the largest of two blocks—the library and reading rooms. It would rest on tall but thin pilotis, so that seen from the Red Square it appeared to float. At right angles, the smaller block of the scientific research institute, also on pilotis, was slotted between the library and the ground creating a miniature galaxy of four hovering bodies, anchored to the center of town by the tenuous link of glittering cables.

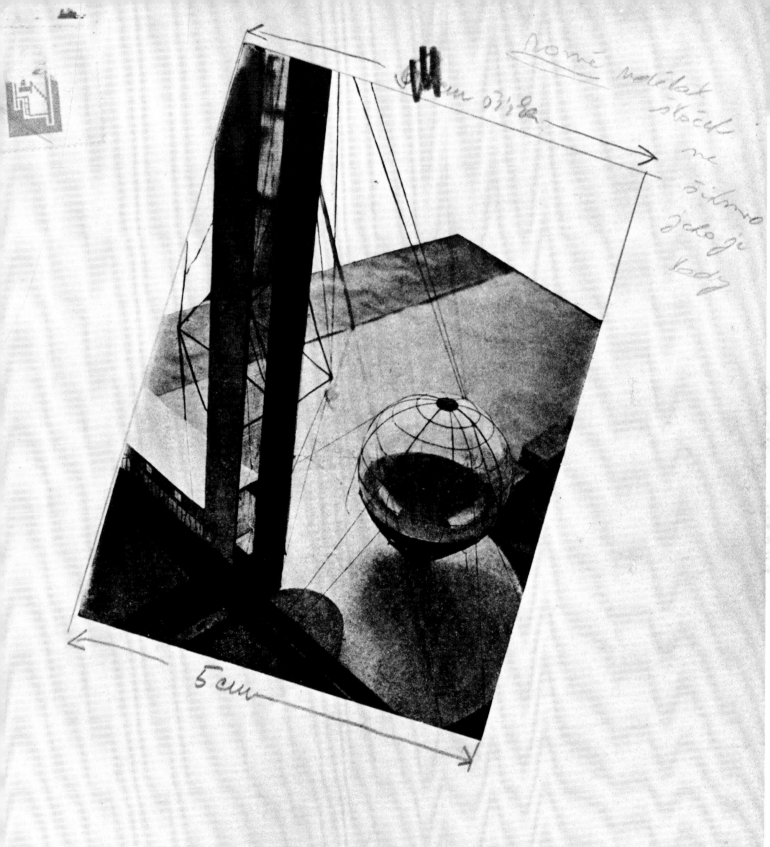

ЛЕОНИДОВ И И

34   *1 Lenin Institute. Moscow, 1927. Ivan Leonidov. Diploma project. General plan.*
2 Lenin Institute. Model. View of auditorium and library.
3 OSA exhibition, 1926. Lenin Institute model in foreground.
4 Lenin Institute. Model. Auditoria and library from above.
5 Lenin Institute. Perspective. Library, bookstack, and monorail.
6 Lenin Institute. Perspective.

3

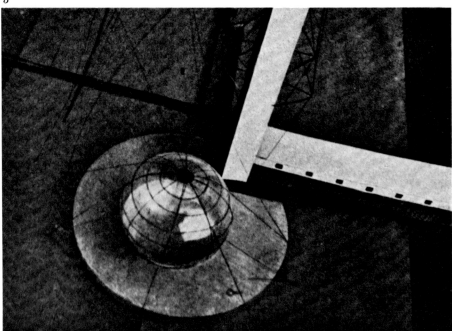

4

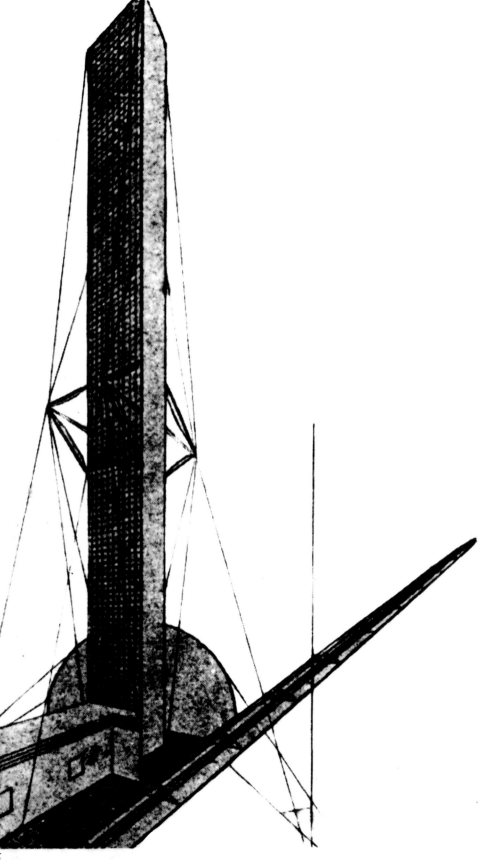

5

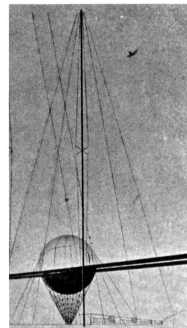

6

36

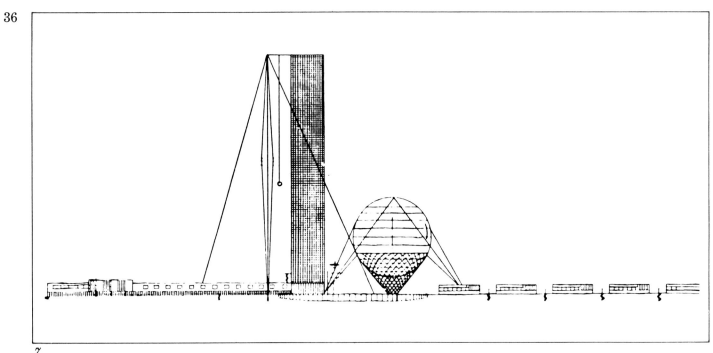

7

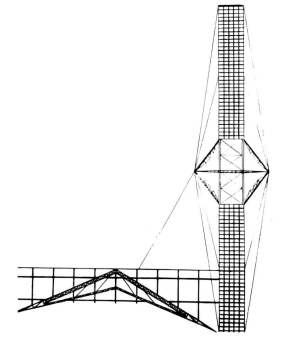

8

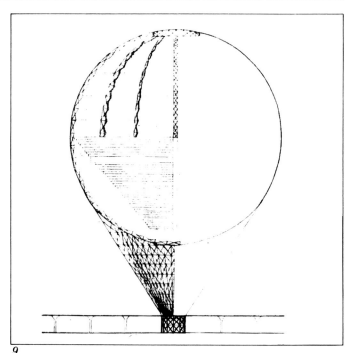

9

37

10

12

11

Film Studio

Moscow 1927

38   These film studios were designed to be located in the Lenin Hills (close to the Lenin Institute project) on the outskirts of Moscow. The complex was arranged to create a variety of "situations" and "environments" to accommodate and stimulate every possible type of cinematic activity.

A railway track connected the main studios with the administration buildings in the distance. This line would be used for the delivery of goods but, more importantly, as a piece of cinematic equipment. Film sets with groups of actors could travel along the railway, on mobile platforms, either toward or away from the camera, past the different environments of a narrow park. Alternatively, a mobile camera could speed past different scenes arranged in the park, while sets of larger format could be erected on the main film lot on the other side of the track.

The truncated cross contained the studios. From its roof, cables would extend to the fringes of the site so camera units, suspended from them, could travel with variable velocity above any part of the lot; or if necessary, fragments of sets could be pulled along cables, at different heights and speeds. Small aircraft could land on the flat roof of this studio and other roofs could be used for shooting open-air sequences.

The L-shaped ground floor of the studio was completely unobstructed and could be divided by sliding partitions into smaller sets, each accessible through a series of stairs ascending from the basement. On the two sides of the lot, steel panels slid away so that action and sets, originating inside the studios, overflowed into the open air.

The basement would contain a collection of decorative facades in all styles, which could be pulled up through slots in the floor and erected where desired; more props could be suspended above the sets, ready to descend when appropriate. A rotating disc inside the studio building, and a second one outside, presented yet more theatrical possibilities.

Electrical installations were located on the top floor of the building; a volume just below this floor would contain four sub-batteries providing light and power for the projects.

The dressing rooms, canteens, and lounges for artists and operators were combined in a separate three-storey building, divorced from the studios so as to afford a calm environment and protect them from fire hazards. This building connected to the main studios by way of three subterranean corridors. Its length was interrupted by three-storey, glazed conservatories. The vast area to the west of the site was provided to accomodate the type of mass activity which the technique of physical montage suggests.

1 Film studio. Moscow, 1927. Ivan
Leonidov. Elevation.
2 Film studio. Elevation.
3 Film studio. Elevation.
4 Film studio. Perspective detail of
interior facade.

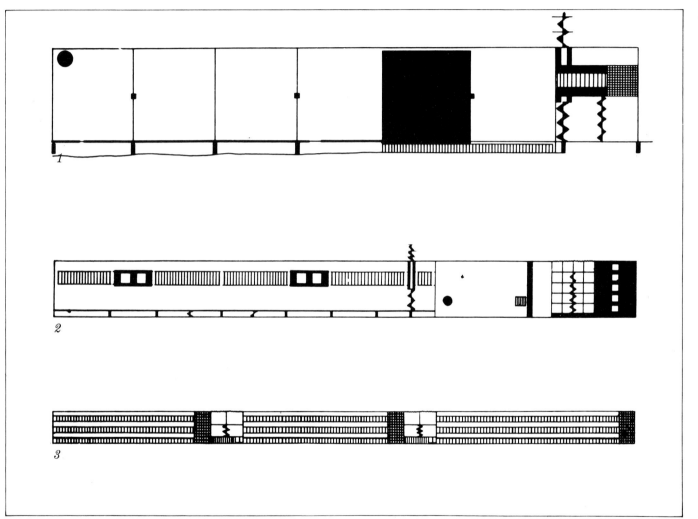

39

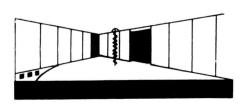

4

5 Film studio. Detail of principal building plan.
6 Film studio. Site plan.
7 Film studio. Axonometric. Components: studio, office, garage, commuter station.

40

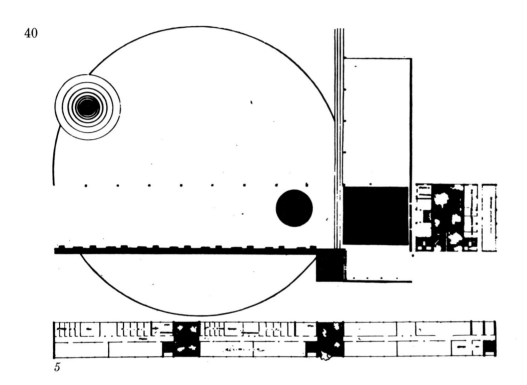

5

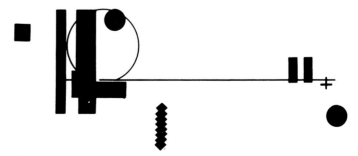

6

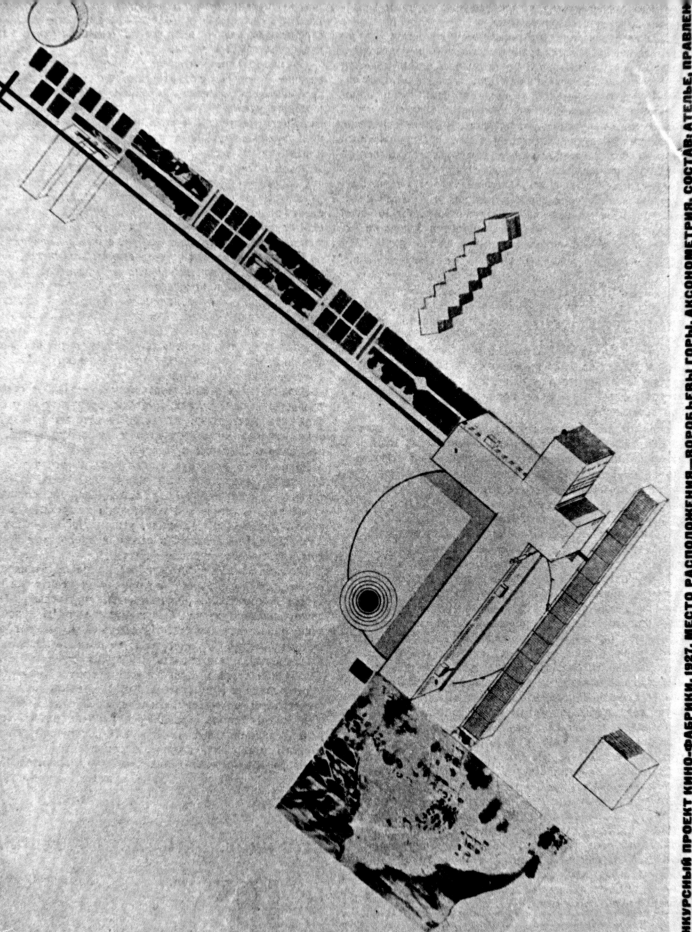

Centrosoyuz

1928

42 The Centrosoyuz (headquarters of the Central Union) was projected in a competition for a rectangular site bounded by two parallel streets, with a section of the urban fabric to be given over to a "green boulevard." The twelve-storey main slab was situated parallel to the projected boulevard and at right angles to the two streets so its ground floor became a covered winter garden/gallery connecting the streets. A separate circular lobby, placed in front of the slab, would serve to attract tourists from the boulevard while an external elevator took them directly up to the roof. The roof-top, equipped with an observation deck, a club room, a cafeteria and a public service point, would provide information on the continuous changes in the Moscow skyline.

The main lobby, situated on the first floor and taking the form of an elongated glass oval, was accessible from three sides: the main stair, a footbridge connecting to the boulevard, and a second footbridge linking the far-sides of the two flanking streets. This lobby was punctured at regular intervals by six banks of paternosters, providing a continuous vertical connection between individual departments. An information counter in the lobby would direct the visitors to the correct "launching-pad" for their ascent through the building. Since the activities were clustered around the points of vertical communication, corridors were virtually abolished.

A single-storey exhibition wing, equipped with a roof garden, would be built at right angles to the lobby and raised on pilotis. The office floors consisted of a few isolated rooms in an otherwise open office landscape (Burolandschaft), punctuated by the six continually chattering groups of paternosters.

Le Corbusier's second, definitive version of the winning design, with its curtain wall facades, suggests the influence of Leonidov's project. Le Corbusier abandoned his earlier use of horizontal strip windows after Leonidov had complained that, "these horizontal bands hurt the eyes, in fact make you see cross-eyed.

1

1 Centrosoyuz. Moscow, 1928. Ivan Leonidov. Model. Front facade.

44 *2 Centrosoyuz. Side elevation.*
3 Centrosoyuz. Ground floor plan
(parkscape and entrance).
4 Centrosoyuz. Schematic plan.
5 Centrosoyuz. Roof plan (roof
garden and running track).

2

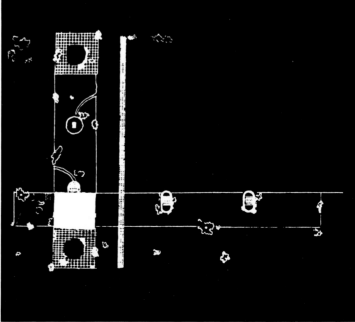

3

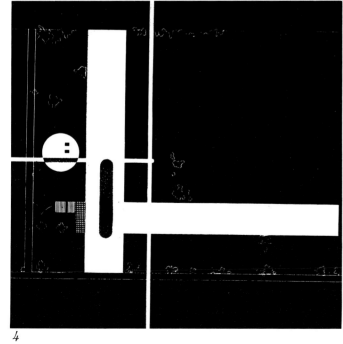

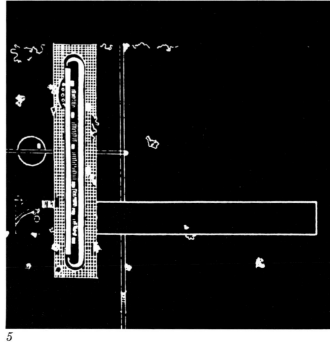

4

5

46

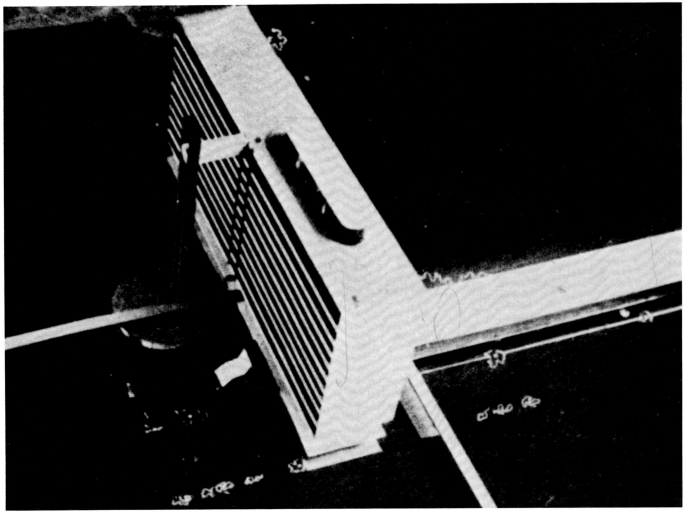

6

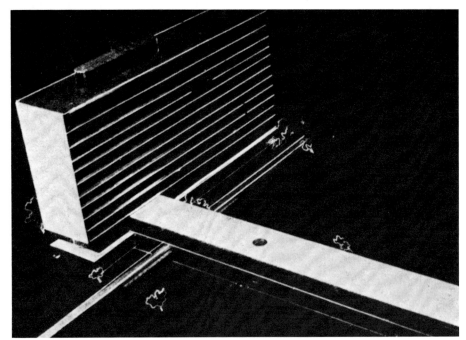

7

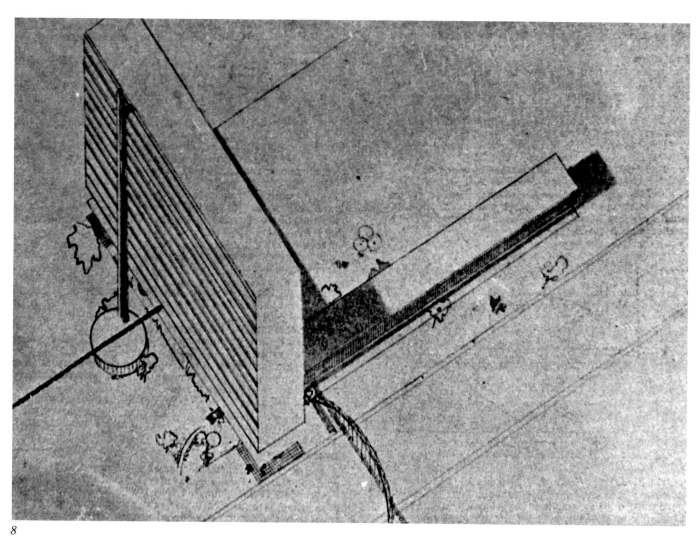

8

6 Centrosoyuz. Model. Front view.
7 Centrosoyuz. Model. Rear view.
8 Centrosoyuz. Axonometric.

Government Center

Alma Ata (Near the Chinese Border) 1928

1 *Goverment Center, Alma Ata, 1928. Ivan Leonidov. Ground floor plan.*
2 *Government Center. Ground floor plan (variation).*
3 *Government Center. Axonometric.*
4 *Government Center. First floor plan.*
5 *Government Center. Front facade elevation.*

48 This three-storey building included a long wing containing government offices and a number of quadrant-shaped lounges for the inevitable waiting periods. In this conventional program, the inventive aspect was mainly concentrated in the short wing which was equipped with a small theater elevated on pilotis, a conference hall, and meeting rooms. All these were raised above the multi-purpose entrance lobby on the ground floor. The end wall of the theater was separated from the outside by a folding screen, so that meetings and performances could be observed from the outside when the stage was transformed into a rostrum. The parking area and the main entrance, connected to a long footpath, were located under the theater which terminated in a roof terrace. Two small gardens were included in the angle where the long and short wings joined. It is more than likely that the facades were inspired by Le Corbusier's Villa Garches, which had then just become known in Moscow.

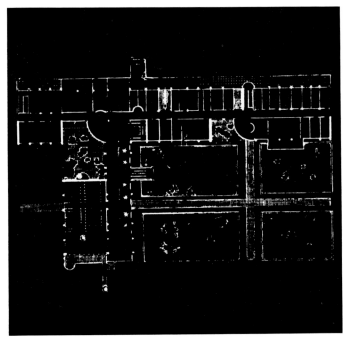

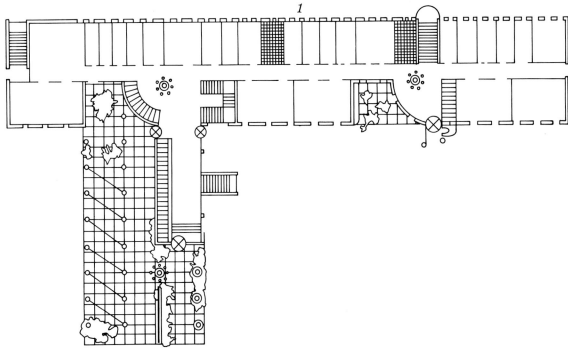

1

2

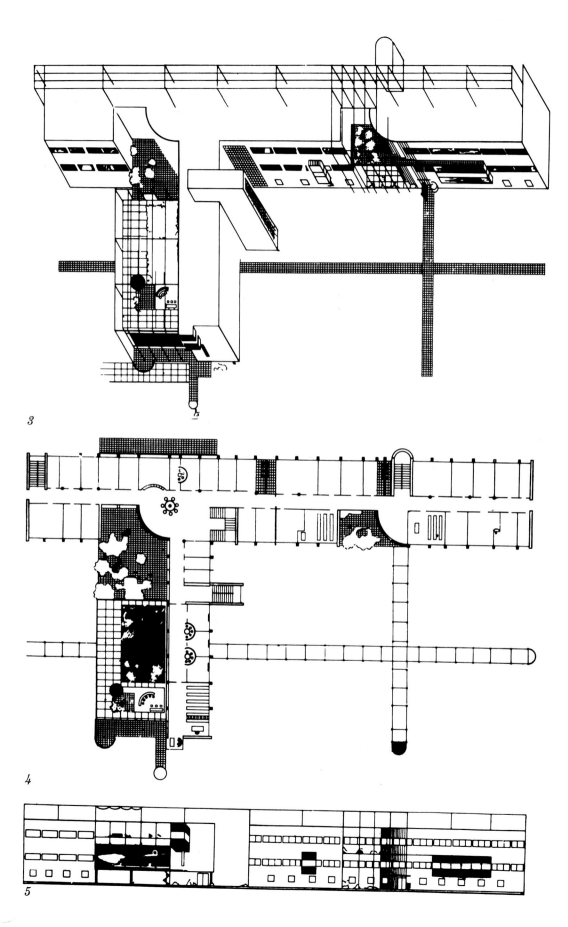

3

4

5

Columbus Memorial

Santo Domingo 1929

50   *"Notes on the Problem of a Memorial" in* SA, *n.4, 1929 served as a source for the following description.*

Leonidov's Columbus Memorial is perhaps his most visionary modern project. The memorial was a proposal for a World Culture Center which would condense all the achievements of world progress in one place, broadcasting the life and role of Columbus and the movement of world history through media.

General plan: The memorial, located twenty meters above sea level, contained an airport on the highest point, a park, and a government building below. The airport, museum, and park were connected by suspended paths; those going from the museum to the meteorological station opened out to rich tropical vistas. Parallel to the cliff, powerful screens would be visible from the sea.

The museum, located in the center of the memorial, stored Columbus's ashes and valuables. It was enclosed with reinforced glass, and strong jets of air acted as "walls." A chapel with a glass cupola on top allowed visitors to view the memorial from all sides.

The port was organized with two 300 meter masts, a lighthouse, and a radio laboratory. All over the world cities were to establish screens in open squares to project Columbus's history (along with contemporary technical achievements), in their respective languages.

The airport, surrounded by covered paths, housed a railway station with embarcation sites and hangars situated below. A floating airbase was to be established in the Atlantic equipped with hangars, hotels, etc.

The Columbus Base (a seaport), located on the Ostam River, included a meteorological station (the barometer of international air and sea information), a scientific research laboratory (the brain of the memorial generating the working plans), radio, film, observatory, institute of interplanetary communication with demonstration field, and a hall for the World Scientific Congress.

1

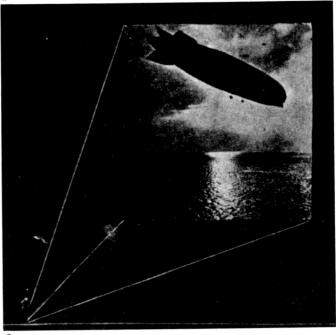

2

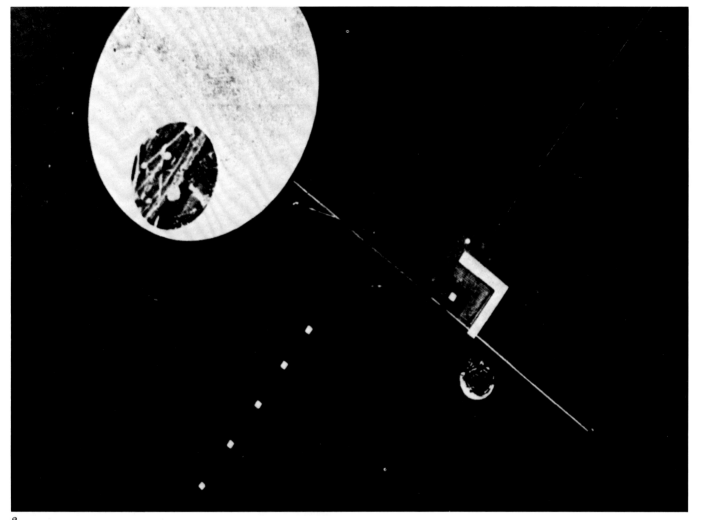

3

1 Columbus Memorial. Santo
Domingo, 1929. Ivan Leonidov.
Front view.
2 Columbus Memorial. Collage.
3 Columbus Memorial. Model. View
from above.
4 Columbus Memorial. Model. View
from above.

4

A New Type of Social Club

1929

52 *Organization of the work of a New Type of Social Club*
The proposed club allocated spaces for the following activities: laboratories, lectures, sports, games, military exercises, museum work, meetings, sociopolitical campaigns, exhibitions, competitions, cinematic exhibitions of new films, planetarium, action campaigns for a new way of life, etc. In addition, a musem and a planetarium were provided.

The club's analytical and mass work would be supervised by trained teachers grouped in a central institute communicating by radio. Lessons would be given via the "long-range transmission of images" (television) and motion pictures. Political and economic news of the day as well as club and scientific institute activities would be flashed on screens or reported over loudspeakers for the purposes of ensuring high quality instruction and the broadest possible diffusion. It would serve as a sort of animated newspaper that no workers' or peasants' collective was without.

In general, the club buildings were of glass skin construction and the supporting structure of reinforced concrete. Up until then the wall had been treated as essentially a thermal, acoustic insulator and a source of light. Due to modern technology, it was no longer necessary for the wall to be a heavy insulating barrier built out of opaque stone or wood, but rather it could be made of transparent glass as a means, Leonidov wrote, of widening the public grasp of environmental dynamics.

Leonidov outlined the elements of this project as follows (in *SA* n.3, 1929, pp.106-113):
1. Botanical winter garden of 2500 square meters, including space for:
a. Experimental botony
b. Zoology
c. Exhibitions
d. Playgrounds, sports, tennis, basketball, croquet, chess, corners for social and political work, etc.
2. Auditorium of 700 square meters for lectures, films, demonstrations, planetariums, meetings, etc.
3. Library
4. Eight scientific laboratories
5. Arenas for gliding and flying, car racing, civil-defence exercises, military games, walking, etc.
6. Gymnasium
7. Sports ground
8. Children's pavilion with play areas and pool
9. Park

1 New Type of Social Club (Variant A). 1929. Ivan Leonidov. Perspective.
2 Social Club (Variant A). Model. View from above.
3 Social Club (Variant B). Ground floor plan.

1

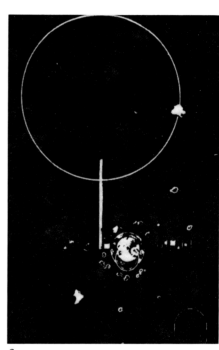

2

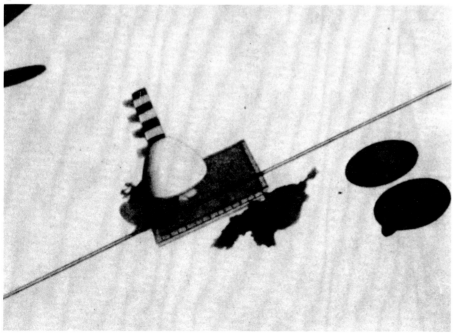

3

54

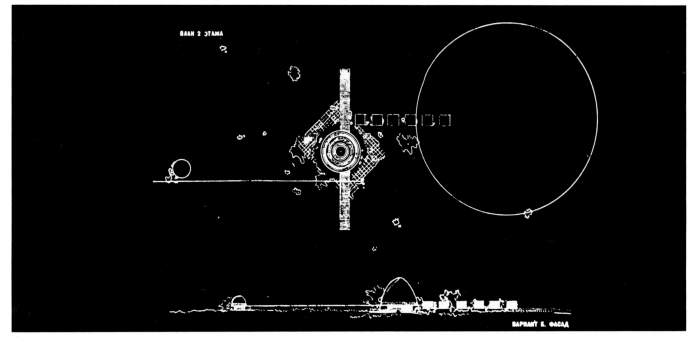

ПЛАН 2 ЭТАЖА

ВАРИАНТ Б. ФАСАД

4

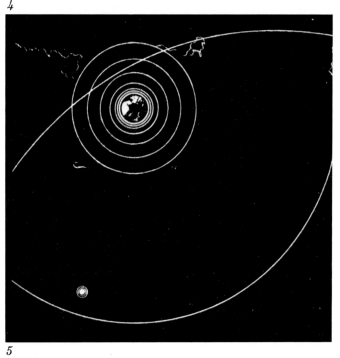

5

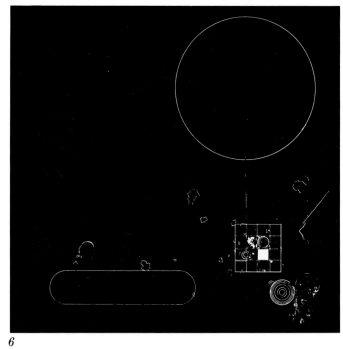

6

4 *Social Club (Variant B). (Top) Plan*
of second floor. (Bottom) Perspective.
5 *Social Club (Variant A). Plan. Net-*
work of cultural centers.
6 *Social Club (Variant A). Ground*
floor plan.
7 *Social Club (Variant A). First floor*
plan, two views of model.

55

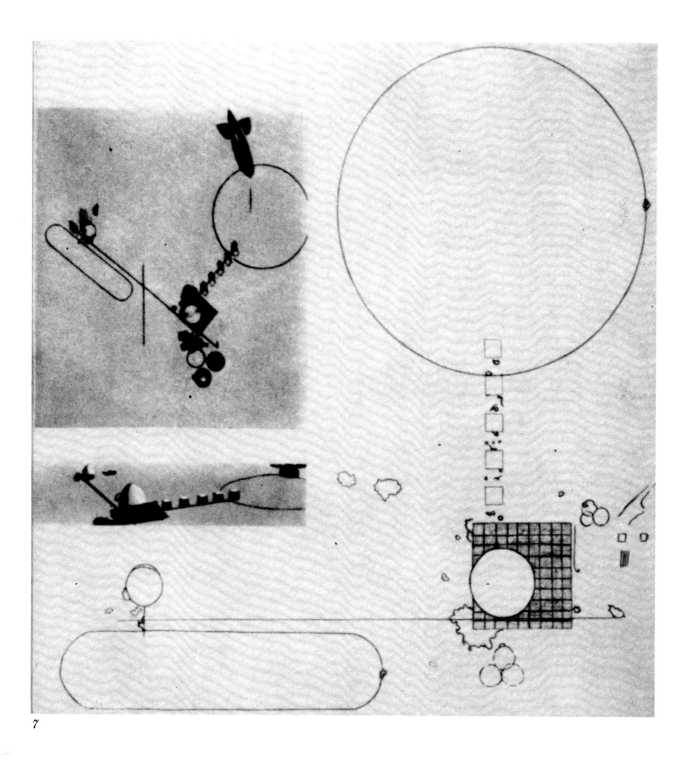

7

The House of Industry

Moscow 1930 Competition Entry

56 This office building was one of the metropolitan components which Leonidov designed with the intention to create a potential think-tank and incubator of progressive ideas.

Explaining his House of Industry, Leonidov writes (in *SA* n.2, 1929):

"Each new structure is a step toward socialism. Work should be organized as a comprehensive system. Characteristics of the old type of structures: enclosed courtyards, no views, small cubicles, too little fresh air, barrack-like corridors, absence of an overall concept."

Based on these concepts for the House of Industry, the rectangular office block with blank end walls and curtain walling in between, and completely glazed curtain-wall facades, makes its debut in the vocabulary of architecture; a type which comes closest to perfection at this moment of its creation.

Inside this minimal transparent enclosure, Leonidov proposed an alternating cycle of intellectual work, physical exercise, and leisure activities—each new effort nullifying the particular type of fatigue left by the previous one—to turn a potential treadmill into a workers' dynamo.

Public facilities (scenic views over Moscow, wintergardens, cafeterias, clubs and exhibitions) would act as magnets to attract passers-by to different levels and locations inside the building, so that these blocks could be incorporated in the general urban experience, and their amenities could be assimilated into the lives of the proletariat.

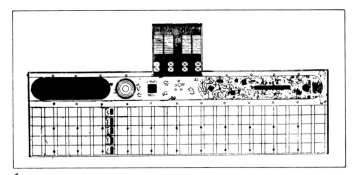

1

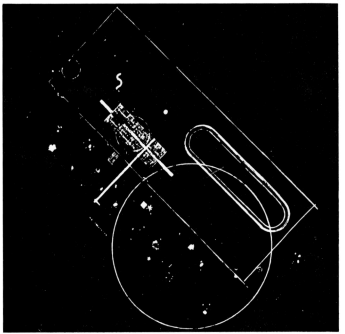

2

1 House of Industry. Moscow, 1930.
Ivan Leonidov. Typical plan for an
office building for the House of
Industry.
2 House of Industry. General plan.
3 House of Industry. Principal
facade elevation.

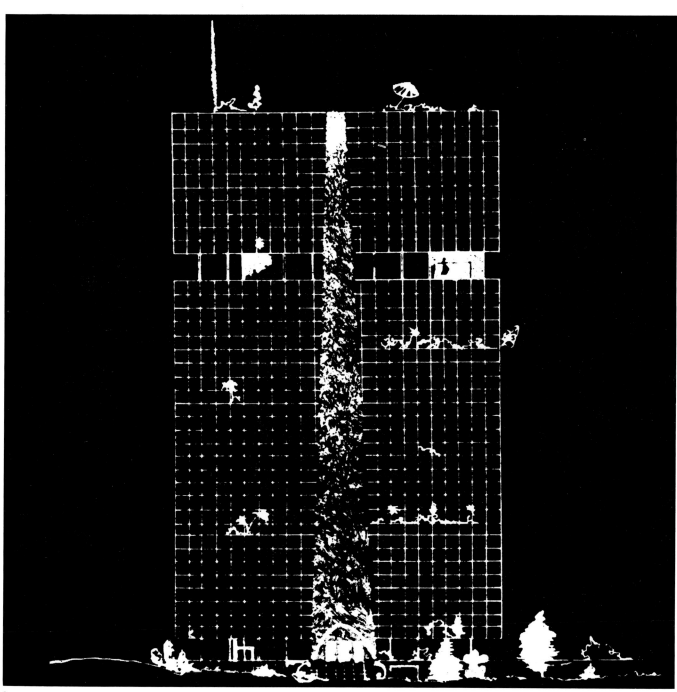

4 House of Industry. Side elevation.
5 House of Industry. Axonometric.

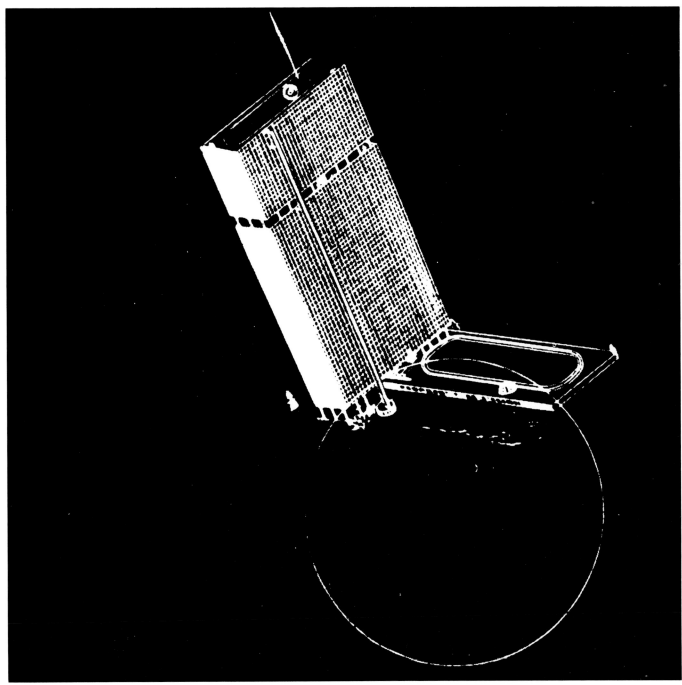

5

Palace of Culture

Moscow 1930

1 Palace of Culture. Moscow, 1930. Ivan Leonidov. Site elevation and general plan. (Left to right) Sectors for scientific and historical research, mass activity, demonstration field, physical culture.

60 In 1930, the workers of a Moscow steel combine organized a competition for a Palace of Culture (headquarters of the "Cultural Revolution") on the site of the former Simonov monastery in Moscow. Theoretically, these conditions were extremely favorable for a definitive statement on Communist culture. The Palace of Culture was to involve the intellectual participation of the workers in the continuous process of political and cultural education, replace a reactionary religious institute, by a secular organization, for the analysis and celebration of life on earth, and rehabilitate a decaying workers' neighborhood through a massive injection of new forms and concepts. But the final brief, drawn up in "countless meetings of workers and their representatives," was an uninspired amalgam of familiar facilities including a cinema, a library, and a theater. Leonidov ignored this brief and pursued his speculations about the club and the invention of collective facilities.

Magomedov writes (in *Building in the USSR* p.128): "The site was divided into four areas to provide for mass demonstrations, physical culture, a sports stadium and science and research activities. Each area had distinctive buildings—a pyramidal sports hall with a swimming pool surrounding it, for instance, and a large glass-domed hall which could be divided with movable partitions. This design was vigorously attacked by members of *VOPRA*, who rejected such experimentation."

The framework of a Russian monastery, or other institutional complexes such as the Kremlin, comprised a large tract of land on which an informally arranged group of buildings of varying importance, life-span, age, style, and architectural virtuosity, would achieve a coherence by virtue of a surrounding wall. In a more formal manner, Leonidov also projected a scattered sequence of activities, facilities, and structures upon a rectangular landing-strip in open space; this zone provided an intense contrast with its densely populated, antiquated surroundings.

ОБЩИЙ ФАСАД

ГЕНЕРАЛЬНЫЙ ПЛАН
научно-исторический сектор

1

Дворец культуры

И. Леонидов

5 1930

'ЕКТУРА

культуры

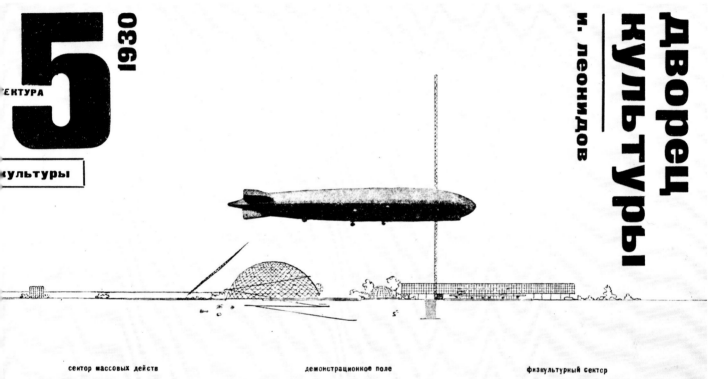

сектор массовых действ   демонстрационное поле   физкультурный сектор

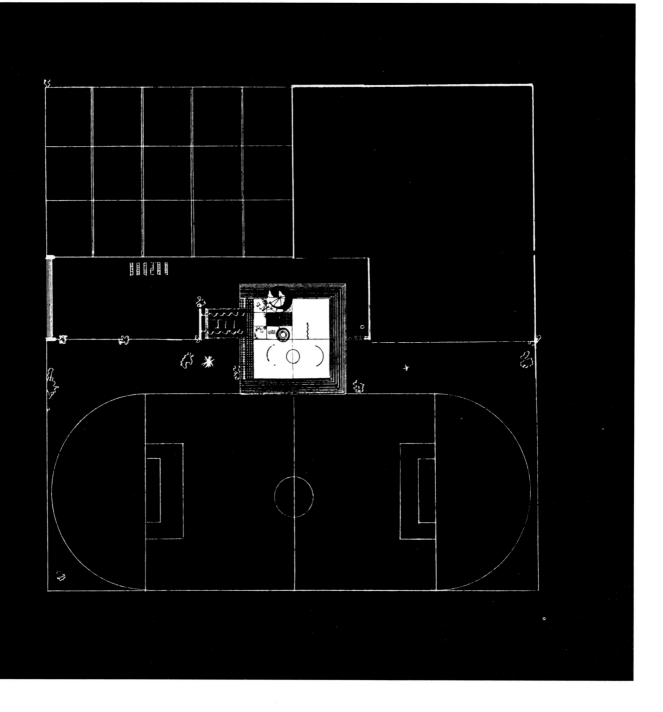

63

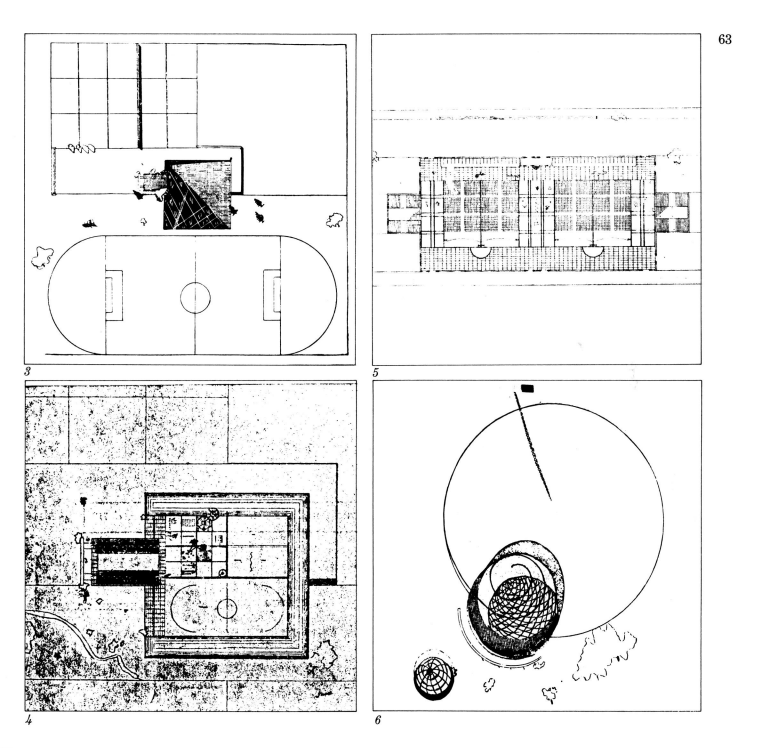

3

5

4

6

7 Palace of Culture. Physical culture center. Facade.
8 Palace of Culture. Mass activity sector. Section.

9 Palace of Culture. Mass activity sector. Plan.
10 Palace of Culture. Theater showing mobile system of circular platforms.

7

8

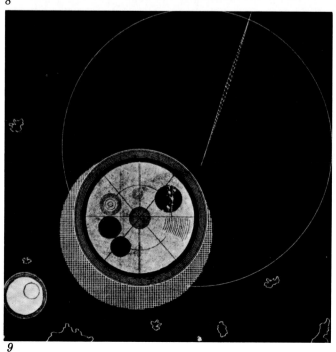

9

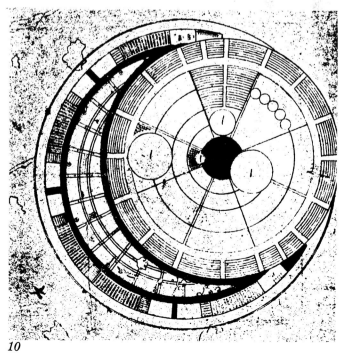

10

11 Palace of Culture. Second phase.
General plan.
12 Palace of Culture. Second phase.
Ground floor plan.

11

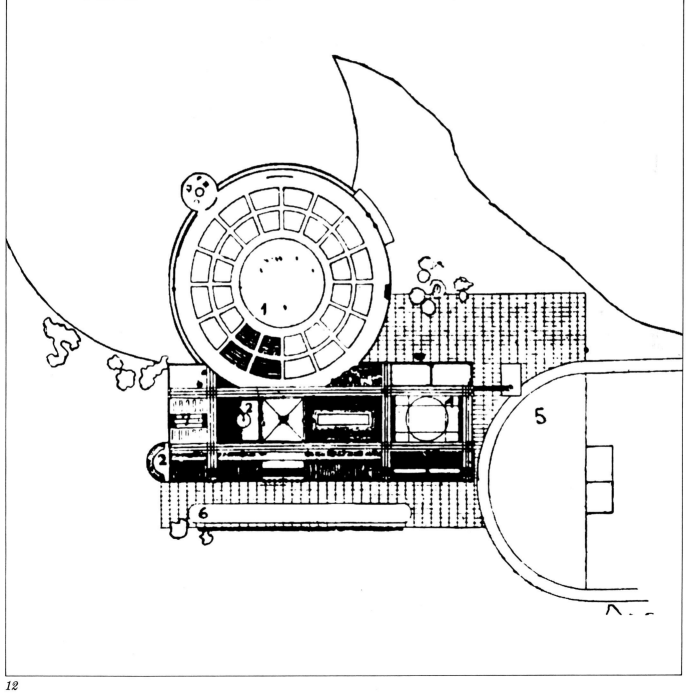

1 Magnitogorsk proposal for a new town. Ural Mountains, 1930. Ivan Leonidov. Propaganda poster: "For Soviet Power dirigible construction."

68 Until 1929, Leonidov had not been involved in the planning of new settlements, or even in the design of housing. By this date, the ideological architectural debate in these areas had become dominated by the controversy between "urbanists" and "de-urbanists." As a result of this polarization, the housing projects of the period came to be formulated in increasingly extreme terms. The urbanists proposed gigantic urban blocks; each one housing a thousand or more inhabitants. This super-collectivized *combinats* were to be equipped with such facilities as nurseries, gymnasia, sports halls, and even with cafeterias where the food was to have been distributed on conveyor belts. Due to the number and density of the populations to be housed, the overriding concern of efficiency led to communal blocks where the quality of life was completely overshadowed by economic considerations. Sabsovitch's project for super-collectivization organized daily life along military lines, where even minutes were rationed out according to a daily timetable, as if time itself had become a rare commodity. Such arrangements frequently presupposed a level of urban sophistication which was totally absent in the actual inhabitants.

The extreme de-urbanist alternative was to be a continuous ribbon of individual cubicles running through the virgin countryside, served at regular intervals by a chain of social amenities. This linear system was assumed to magically dissolve existing cities wherever it encountered them. While the dehumanizing size of the first solution was totally unacceptable, the sub-density and extreme dispersal of the second would have obviously condemned its inhabitants to a level of isolation which was utterly anti-social.

"The problem of the socialist settlement, and especially that of the commune house, has not yet been solved. The standard house-communes, architectural copies of old prototypes such as hotels or barracks, cannot respond to the new organization of society." *(Doma-Kommuny,* Moscow, 1931.)

When Leonidov established criteria for the Leningrad student commune, he insisted that the prime aim was "first, a new social concept, and second, its translation into architecture."

In Magnitogorsk, the population of the commune was to be subdivided into smaller groups. Each communal house was designed to house sixteen people, while groups of eight such houses made a neighborhood of 128 people. There were to be individual rooms in which to sleep, work, and relax, and communal areas for hygiene, leisure and eating. In the immediately surrounding parkscape, the following amenities would also be provided: nurseries, a kindergarten, a central club for cultural activities, a cinema, a meeting hall/auditorium, and fields for physical exercise and for mass demonstrations.

Leonidov was also to project intriguing alternatives for the organization of the standard neighborhood five-by-five square block. In some cases the five-by-five sector would become the site for two thirteen–storey towers using the same cruciform plan and section as the low–rise two–storey communal dwellings. With each tower, accomodating 96 people, the total population per sector was 192. Each sector was provided with its own boating/swimming pool which was centrally located in the twin tower solution and asymmetrically situated in the low-rise pattern.

The settlement of sectors were also designed for gradual occupation; and Leonidov shows a version in which the sector is still partly given over to horticulture.

The following aims were sought in this organization:
1. The arrangement of a group living in such a way as to avoid enforced socialization and excessive densities which would inhibit the spontaneity of daily life;
2. to establish a close relationship between architecture and nature thereby abolishing private lots and gardens;
3. to provide a maximum freedom for living arrangements and for interpersonal relationships;
4. to create a state of resilience (*élan de vie*) through the planned organization of a given territory.

за советское
мощное
дирижаблестроение

2

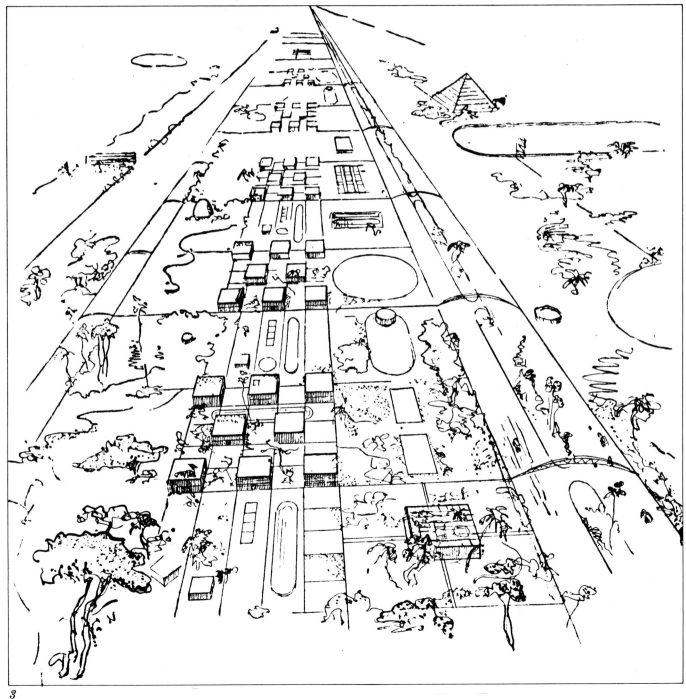

2 Magnitogorsk. Elevation.
3 Magnitogorsk. Linear perspectival
plan for residential sector.
4 Magnitogorsk. Residential sector
for low-rise buildings. Axonometric.

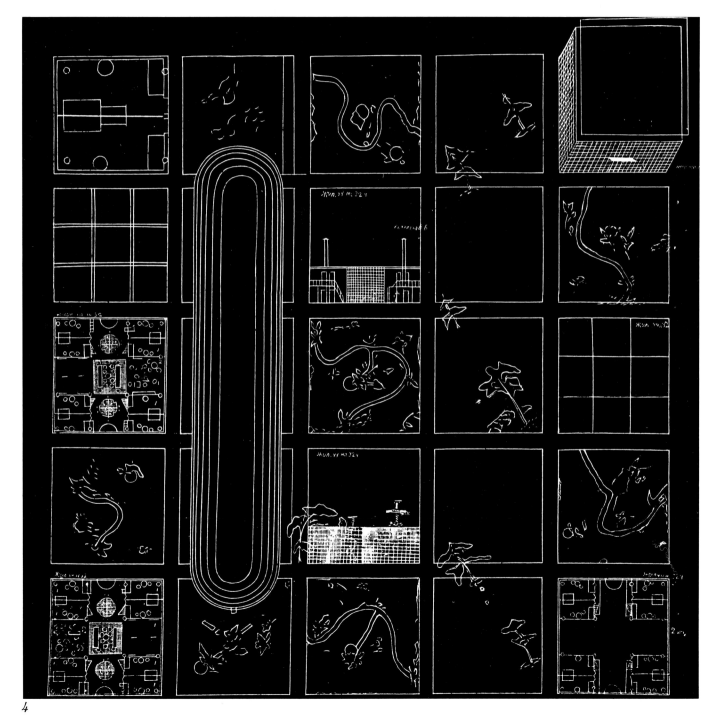

72

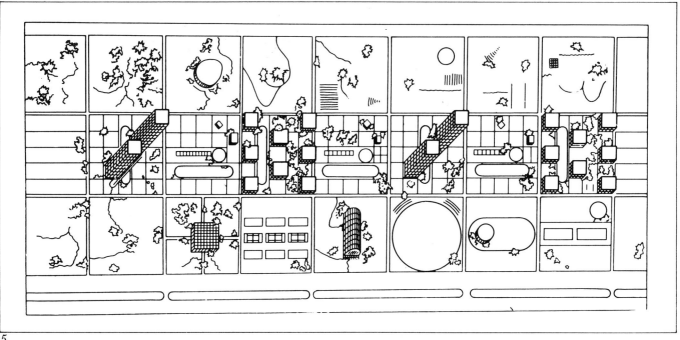

5

6

5 *Magnitogorsk. Plan. Central band composed of alternating low and high-rise housing, bordered by public facilities.*

6 *Magnitogorsk. Detail of Model. View from above.*

7 *Magnitogorsk. Alternating system of residential low-rise and high-rise buildings. Perspective detail.*

8 *Magnitogorsk. Sector of plan showing its division into five separate zones. The first two zones are devoted to parkscape; the next two to sports facilities, including playcourts and boating pool. The final zone is given over to horticulture. Also, plans and elevations of standard building types are shown.*

7

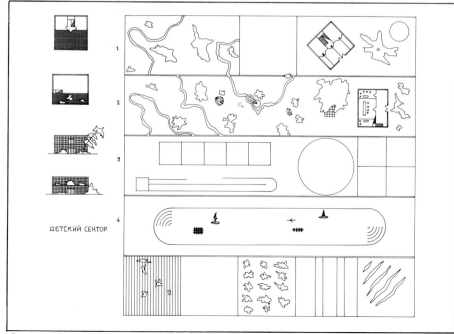

ДЕТСКИЙ СЕКТОР

8

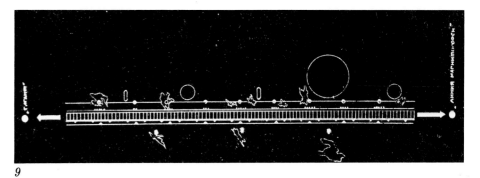

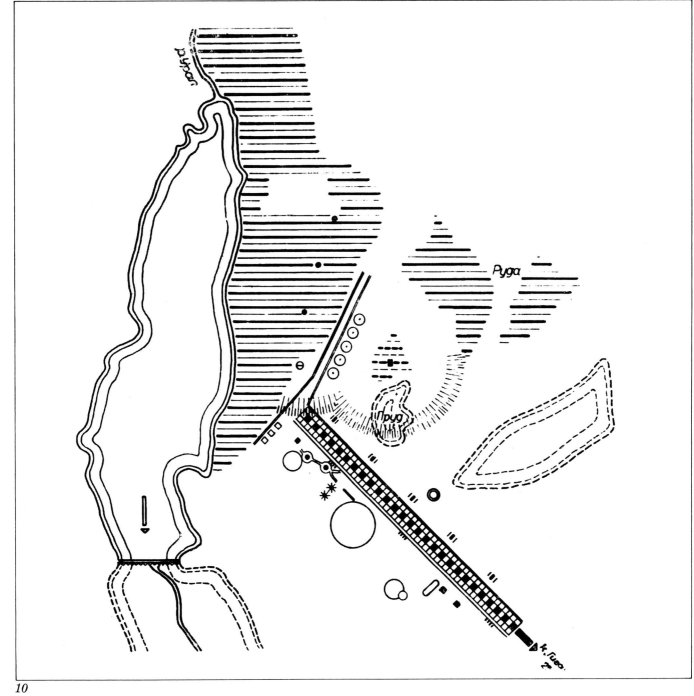

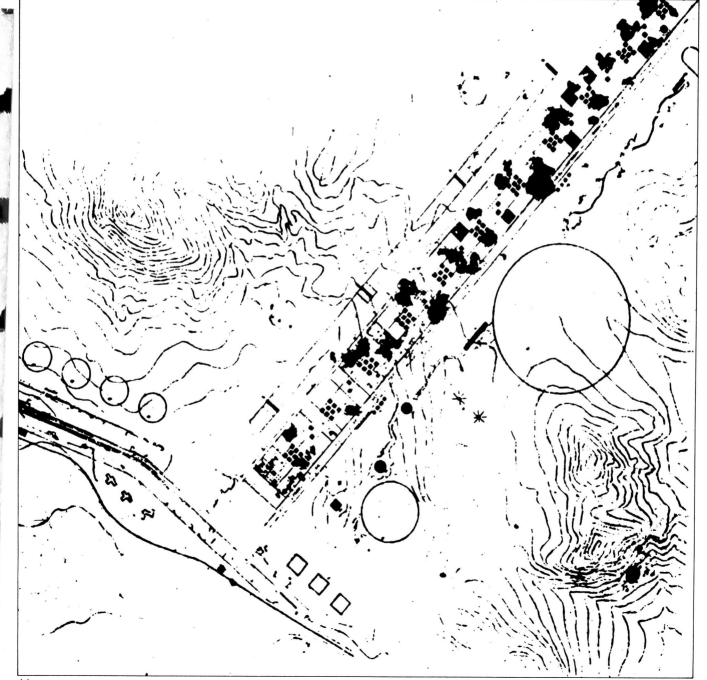

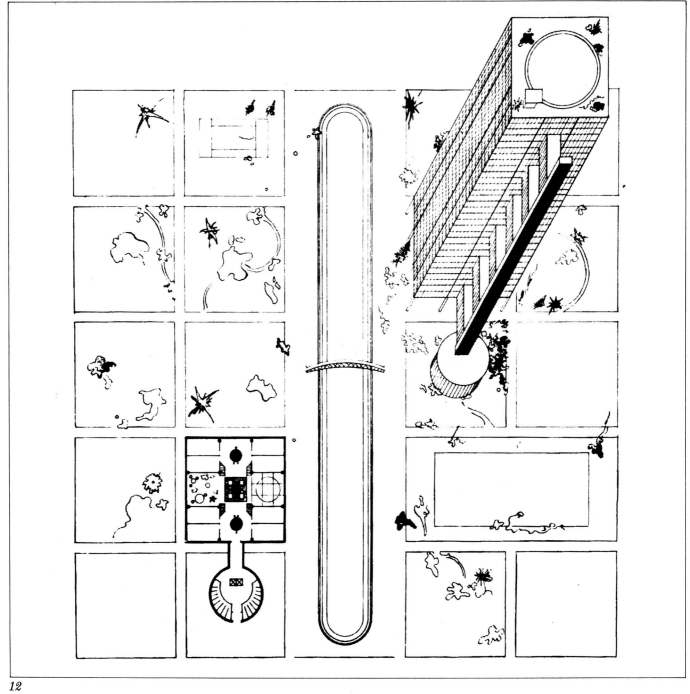

12 Magnitogorsk. Central residential
band. Axonometric detail.
13 Magnitogorsk. Residential sector
with low-rise buildings. General
plan.

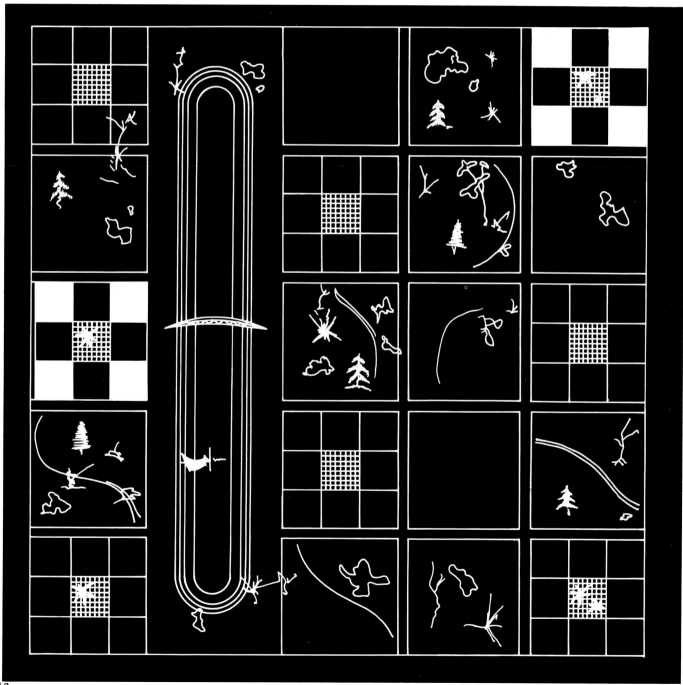

14 Magnitogorsk. Prototypical two-storey residence. Ground floor partitioned into eight individual cells, terrace, winter garden, sports facilities, etc.
15 Magnitogorsk. Prototypical two-storey residence. Section showing stairs.

16 Magnitogorsk. Prototypical two-storey residence. Elevation.
17 Magnitogorsk. Prototypical residential interior. Perspective.

78

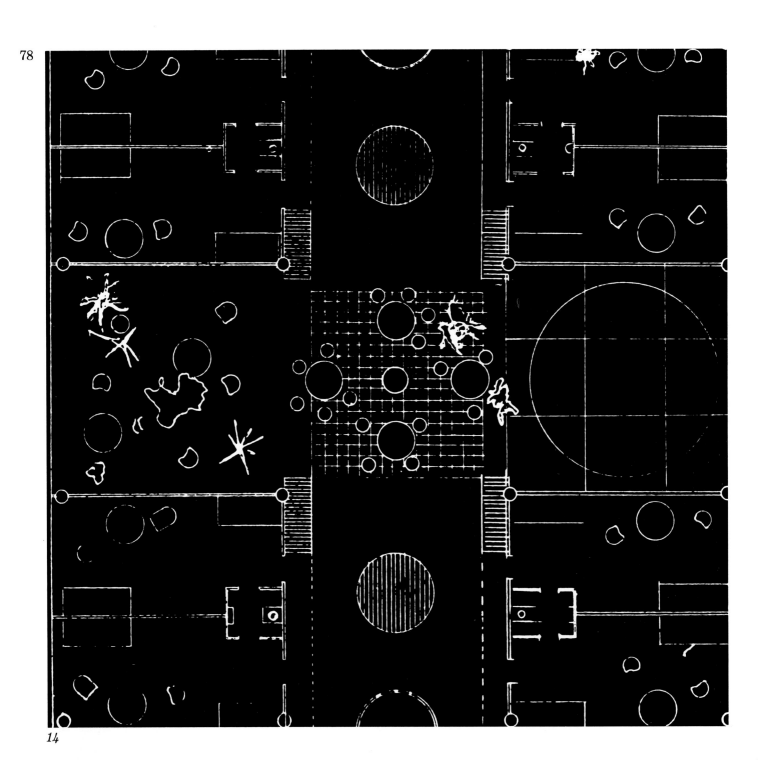

14

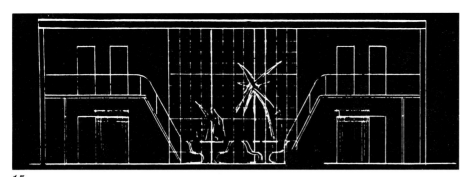

15

16

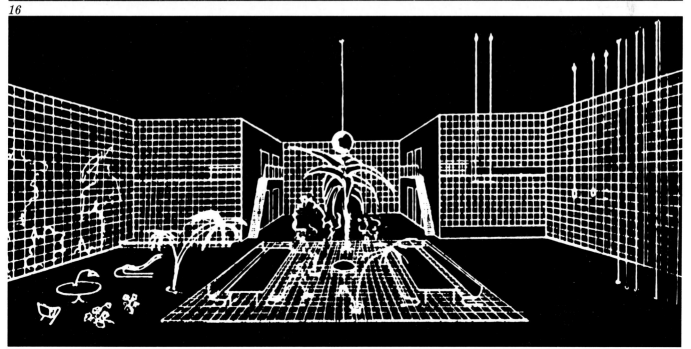

17

Hermitage Park

Moscow 1932

80 The Hermitage Park project was designed for the short-term (five years) rehabilitation of the small Hermitage Park in an old workers' quarter which was to be totally reconstructed according to "the great new principles of building." The central feature of the rectangular site was a two-dimensional suprematist composition of flowerbeds and a round basin intersected by straight, tapering, twisting, circular paths; these ensured a serendipitous distribution of strollers throughout the small park. To the right, an elongated restaurant, with space for 104 tables and a roof terrace for 100 tables, was to be built against the blank wall of the office building. The opposite edge was defined by a sequence of semi-circular bays used for chess and drinking pavilions. Each bay had its own timber statue—a cube, an icosahedron, or a giant chess knight—all painted in bright colors. An open-air theater, at one end of the site, would be used for lectures, musical performances and, by virtue of an eight by eight grid on the stage, for giant chess exhibitions made with "living pieces."

At the other end of the park a timber structure, eleven meters high, served as a "canvas" for a colorful "neon painting" of flowers and trees. At night, geometric, neon-lit illuminations within the flowerbeds would heighten their colors to an unnatural intensity.

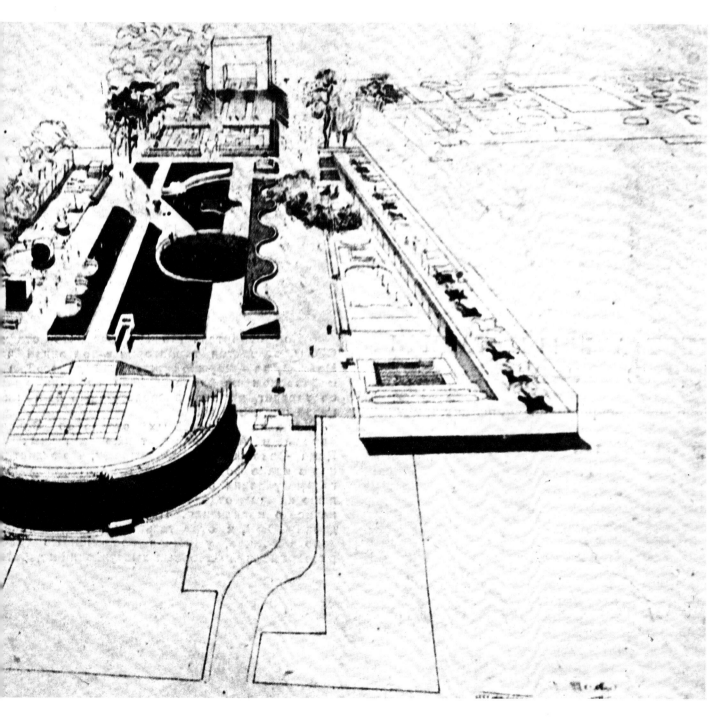

Crimea Coast

1939-1940

Note: the Great Artek project and the Crimea Coast proposals are not shown in this catalogue. They will be extensively documented in a forthcoming study on Leonidov to be written by Oorthuys and Koolhaas.

82 From 1934 until the Second World War, Leonidov worked in the Atelier for Architectural Projects at the Ministry of Heavy Industry—the central planning body for the entire Soviet Union. His friend and admirer, Moisei Ginzburg, was the director of the Atelier. For Leonidov, the Atelier provided an enclave of sympathy and respect in a climate which was otherwise hostile.

The main task of the Ginzburg workshop was the transformation of the Crimea Coast—famous for its climate, subtropical vegetation, and arcadian landscapes—into a Soviet Riviera. The overall project comprised the extensive development of vacation camps, youth hostels, sanatoria, union recreational compounds, parks, open-air theaters, marinas, cultural facilities, together with villas for government officials. In short, it was to be a Communist pleasure zone for deserving citizens.

The architectural strategy for this colonization was simple; a continuous boulevard ran along the Black Sea beaches and the natural phenomena of the site—hilltops, slopes, ridges, ravines, mountain streams—would be exploited for their location to accomodate the individual institutions. An intricate web of footpaths, stairs, amphitheaters, and cablecars would be woven over the hills to tie the institutions, scattered over the area like a rainfall of architectural meteorites, back into these landscapes.

Great Artek
The Great Artek occupied a two-mile stretch of the Crimea Coast with a population of 2250 (1200 in winter). Pioneers from all over the Soviet Union would spend several weeks here both as a reward for outstanding performance in the Pioneer Movement (a Socialist version of the Scout movement in the West), and a period of training and education. Upon their return into society, the young Pioneers, charged like small ideological batteries, would serve as models of perfection.

The Great Artek's transient population, in Leonidov's opinion too amorphous to be organized into a single organism, would be distributed over five separate camps housing 450 Pioneers with each camp having its own architectural identity. Small sub-groups of thirty to forty Pioneers were to be the basic social and architectural unit within these camps. According to Leonidov, this size would encourage a meaningful sense of group membership and idenfitication in order to enhance involvements with larger collectives.

Each unit consisted of some eight to ten dormitories arranged around a plaza with a camp fire located in the center. A Pioneer House and service facilities included a social club, dining hall, auditorium for 400, and kitchens, infirmary etc. With the addition of a park equipped with sports facilities surrounding the entire complex, the camp was complete.

A network of footpaths, stairs and gardens connected the five camps to the beaches and the main boulevard, and thus to each other. Scattered through the gardens were a series of intimate social oases—unusual forms and statues, pools, amphitheaters; the familiar fragments of Leonidov's fantasies which were certain to appeal to the young if not to adults.

A miniature railway connected the five camps to a collective center for the entire community to be located on a prominent ridge dominating the area. From this point, a sequence of public facilities descended toward the Black Sea.

Topped by a crown-like theater and assembly hall for 1500, there was an open-air amphitheater in front of the crown, and a small group of exhibition facilities. A giant staircase-stadium, cut through the ridge, faced a large oval arena used for performances, demonstrations, and games; the bonfire of Socialist joy was at its center. Beyond, on axis, lay a small harbor on the Black Sea.

In the morning, all units were to assemble in front of their dormitories to exercise and receive their instructions for the daily program. The regimen of activities would be a blend of sports, games, and education in which the categories would be overlapped and ultimately unified. The essential arena of this fusion was a "World Park"—a gigantic map of the world implanted on the hills, to the left and right, of the collective center.

1 Ordjonikidze Sanitorium, am-
phiteater, stairs, and landscaping.
Kislovodsk on Crimea Coast,
1930-1940. Ivan Leonidov; the
Sanitorium designed by M. Ginz-
burg. Photograph of main staircase
in front of the medical hospital.
2 Ordjonikidze Sanitorium. Detail of
arcade in main staircase.

83

1

2

3

Crimea Coast

Additional schemes drawn by Leonidov, for the Crimea Coast, showed a cultivated strip of parkscape and a sequence of pavilions, colonnades, bridges, and fountains situated in the original terrain. A large pyramid, in one instance, housed a clubhouse-*cum*-swimming pool for indoor winter activities.

Two adjacent hilltops were initial inspirations for the design. The highest would be planted with three rings of scarlet flowers increasing in density toward the top; the second would be planted with blue flowers. A Roman bridge crossed the ravine that separated them, while in the space between, a large gilded amphitheater would be carved out of a slope facing the Black Sea. On the irregular plateau, which tops the Red Hill, was a temple-like museum—a huge sculpture of crystal with waterworks and round, square, and oval podia for different kinds of performances featuring music, gymnastics, dance, etc. Footpaths descended from the twin hilltops toward the amphitheater. A more formal approach, interrupted by a sequence of three differently-shaped open-air "rooms", descended toward the Black Sea, crossed a small river, and connected the entire complex to a circus on the boulevard.

Kislovodsk

The sanatorium complex at Kislovodsk, basically designed by Ginzburg, was the only real structure to be realized after four years of intense speculative activity. Leonidov designed its gardens and turned the slope facing the Black Sea into a kind of "social" cascade, a theme which was recurrent in all of his Crimea projects. Thus we find here the familiar network of footpaths, stairs, steps, niches, benches, verandas, and fountains which gradually progress downhill and, in this case, culminate in the intertwined cones of an amphitheater. It is the only project Leonidov ever built and, since it was designed overnight, each detail was determined on the site as the building progressed. Ultimately this design proved to be very popular with the patients; its fountain, crescent-shaped benches, flared columns, and bristling pine-trees, all served to evoke an architecture that might have been.

*3 Ordjonikidze Sanitorium. Detail of
amphitheater in main staircase.
4 Ordjonikidze Sanitorium. Aerial
view of main staircase and site.
5 Ordjonikidze Sanitorium. Detail of
staircase.*

4

5

Dom Narkomtiazhprom

Red Square, Moscow 1933 Competition Entry

86

1

This project was designed during the initial period of Leonidov's enforced retreat; "bad Leonidovism" was still a controversial issue and the official architectural emphasis was shifting away from Constructivism toward a politicized amalgam of Classical and Vernacular styles, according to the doctrine of Socialist Realism. In 1933, the Soviet government organized a competition for the Dom Narkomtiazhprom (Ministry of Heavy Industry), the center for all planning activity then being carried out in the Soviet Union. The conditions also required a proposal for a large area east of the Kremlin.

A gargantuan office building was to be inserted in the heart of Moscow east of the Red Square, facing the exotic ensemble of the Kremlin, Lenin's newly built mausoleum; an accomodation which threatened to crush the delicacy of St. Basil's Cathedral by its bulk alone.

To locate an important building on such a symbolically nationalist site was an attempt to incorporate the glory of the past into the mythology of the Revolution through architecture.
Commenting on his proposal, Leonidov wrote:
"Until now, the Kremlin and St. Basil's Cathedral have been the architectural center of Moscow. Obviously, the erection of an enormous new complex on the Red Square will affect the status of the individual monuments which constitute this center. I feel that the architecture of the Kremlin and St. Basil's Cathedral should be subordinated to the Dom Narkomtiazhprom, that the new building should occupy the central position in the city.

The architecture of the Red Square and the Kremlin is like a subtle and majestic music. To introduce new instruments of a colossal order of scale and volume into this symphony is only permissible if this instrument will dominate and surpass, in architectural quality, all other objects of this composition. Not pomposity, not inflated falsehood of forms and details, but simplicity, severity, balanced dynamism and massiveness should determine the design for Dom Narkomtiazhprom. In the composition, historical elements should be subservient to the dominant object through the principle of artistic contrast."

3 Dom Narkomtiazhprom. Perspective with St. Basil's Cathedral in foreground.
4 Dom Narkomtiazhprom. General plan.
5 Dom Narkomtiazhprom. Model.
6 Dom Narkomtiazhprom. Site plan.

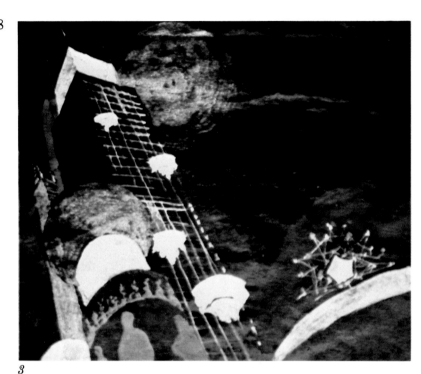

3

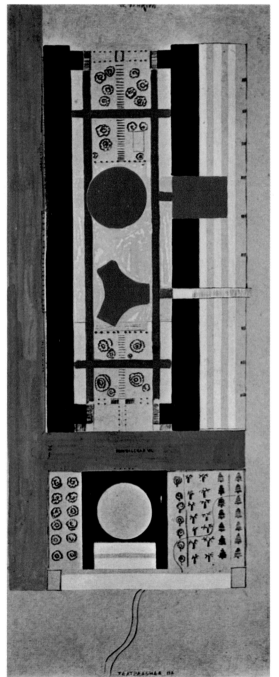

4

The Dom Narkomtiazhprom model
was researched and built by Jay
Johnson (assisted by James Vasquez)
in 1977, and is presently in the collection of the Museum of Modern
Art, New York.

5

6

7

8

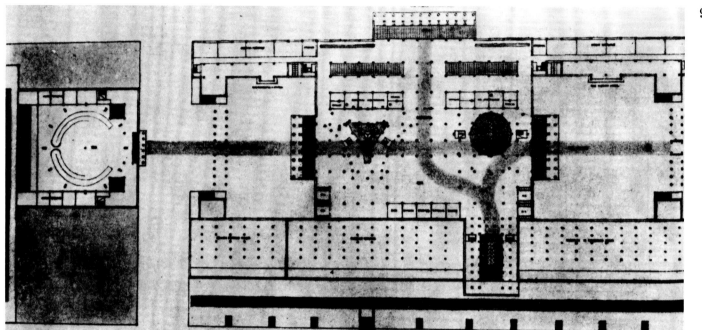

9

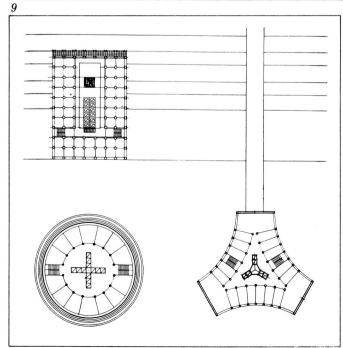

10

11 Dom Narkomtiazhprom. Collage of Kremlin with towers.
12 Dom Narkomtiazhprom. Elevation.

13 Dom Narkomtiazhprom. Sketch. Elevation.
14 Dom Narkomtiazhprom. Sketch of Kremlin with towers in the distance.

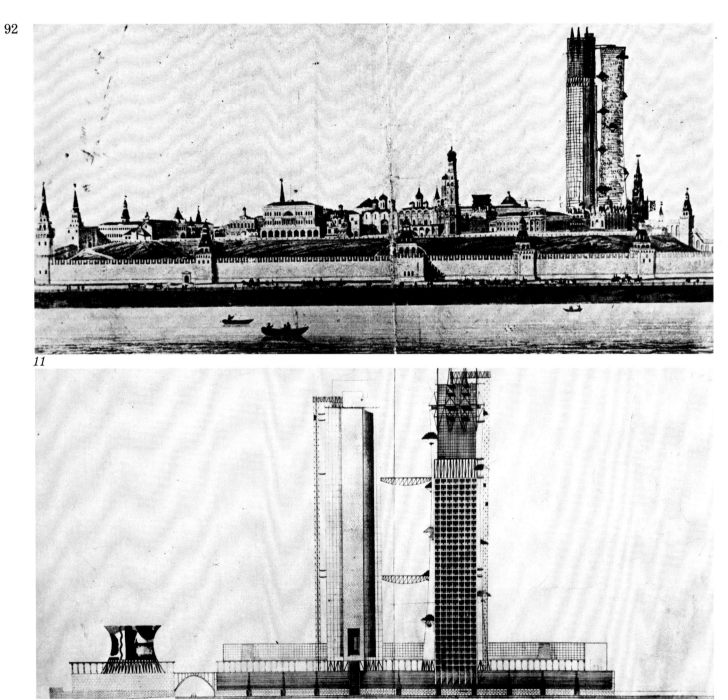

11

12

13

14

The City of the Sun

1947-1959

94 While working on the Crimea projects, Leonidov had the first notions of an ideal city. He projected an international model of a harmonious future for humankind. This project, The City of the Sun, was intended as a synthesis of all his previous projects and ideas, as an architectural condensation of his philosophy. Leonidov worked on the notion of The City of the Sun from the period of the Second World War until his death in 1959; during this period the Soviet Union euphemistically described his architecture as his "hobby". There is no definitive City of the Sun project, but three designs—one for Flower Island situated near Kiev, the United Nations skyscraper complex projected for an island in the Indian Ocean, and the Moscow World's Fair—are fragmentary elaborations of the original concept.

The United Nations
If Flower Island was the new school, the United Nations project was the prototype for The City of the Sun Center, where the architecture was at its most intense. It was designed as an accumulation of institutions, public facilities, and social condensers. After a war, which would have reduced a muted technological optimism, it could serve as a zone for memorials, statues, mementoes, and other symbols relating to collective anxieties and aspirations.

Leonidov, with a political clairvoyance inspired by his life-long love for Chinese and Indian architecture, considered an Asian location an essential condition for building the United Nations and, hence, selected an island in the Indian Ocean. Like his project for the World's Fair, every nation in the world could build its own pavilion on this island as a statement of its most typical ideals and traditions.

Moscow World's Fair
Leonidov's proposal for a World's Fair in Moscow was the final incarnation of The City of the Sun idea. The towers were even more flamboyant that those of the Dom Narkomtiazhprom project; a gilt balloon hovered above the onion-like spires of St. Basil's Cathedral while statues directed their gaze to the walls of the Kremlin. The national pavilions were scattered along the banks of the Moskva River. Finally, a ring of international institutes encircled the city.

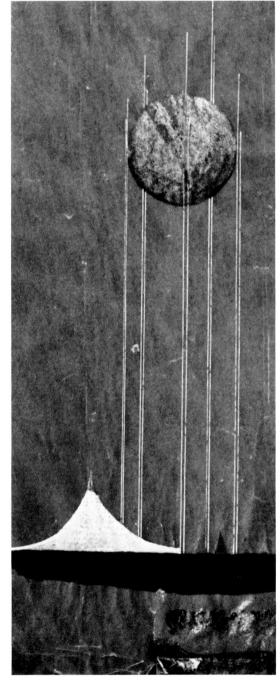

1

1 City of the Sun. 1947-1959. Ivan Leonidov. Paper and ink collage of one building for the United Nations complex.
2 City of the Sun. Conceptual sketches.

Flower Island
Flower Island was to be a park: "a collective place of creation, meditation and rest" where the inhabitants of Kiev— children and adults—could retire "after the inevitable work, to do the work they loved." This "beloved work" was the creation, amid the spontaneous

natural environment of the island, of a second, synthetic nature. It would take form in the cultivation of mutant vegetations, importation of exotic plants, creation of abstract or figurative flowerbed paintings, drawings, mathematical measurements, and plant-like sculptures made from coral.

96

*3 City of the Sun. Sketch of building
complex for the United Nations.*

Bibliography

Writings by Ivan Leonidov

1927
"Institut Lenina. Pojasnitel'naja zapiska k proektu." (The Lenin Institute. Explanatory notes on the project.") *Sovremennaya Arkhitektura*, n.4-5, pp.119-124.

1928
"Kinofabrika. Pojasnitel'naja zapiska k proektu." ("Cinematographic studies. Explanatory notes on the Film Studios.") *Sovremennaya Arkhitektura*, n.1, p.6-8.

1929
"Proekt kluba novogo socialnogo tipa. Pojasnitel'naja zapiska k proektu." ("A New Type of Social Club. Explanatory notes on the project.") *Sovremennaya Arkhitektura*, n.3, pp.103-109.

"Questions posed to Comrade Leonidov after his report of the First Congress of OSA, and his answers." *Sovremennaya Arkhitektura*, n.3, pp.110-111.

"Zapiska k probleme pamajatnika." ("Notes on the problem of the Columbus Memorial monument.") *Sovremennaya Arkhitektura*, n.4, p.148.

1930
"Proekt socialisticeskogo rasselenija pri Magnitogorskom chimiko-metallurgiceskom kominate. Pojasnital'naja zapiska k proektu." ("Project of the urban settlement of the metallurgic-chemical complex of Magnitogorsk. Explanatory notes on the project.") *Sovremennaya Arkhitektura*, n.3, pp.1-5.

"Dom promyslennosti. Pojasnitel'naja zapiska k proektu." ("House of Industry. Explanatory notes on the project.") *Sovremennaya Arkhitektura*, n.4, p.1.

"Dvorec Kultury. Pojasnitel'naja zapiska k proektu." ("Palace of Culture. Explanatory notes on the project.") *Sovremennaya Arkhitektura*, n.5, pp.1-3.

1931
"K proektam Vyssevo chudozestvenno-techniceskogo instituta (nyne Vasi)." ("On the projects of the technical-artistic higher institute, now Vasi.") *Doma-Kommuny*, Leningrad, p.29.

1933
"Kacestvo architecktury na vyssuju stupen." ("The quality of architecture at an elevated level.") *Strojetel'stvo Moskvy*, n.4, p.13.

1934
"Palitra Architektora." ("The Architect's Palette.") *Arkhitektura Sssr*, n.4, pp.32-33.

"Konkurs forproektov Domma Narkomtjazproma v Moskve. Proekt I.I. Leonidova. Pojasnitel'naja zapiska k proekty." ("Competition of projects for the Narkomtiazhprom Commissariat in Moscow. Project of I.I. Leonidov. Explanatory notes on the project.") *Arkhitektura Sssr*, n.10, pp.14-15.

1936
"Attendance at a discussion on works of architecture and painting at the House of Pioneers and Octoberites in Moscow." *Arkhitektura Sssr*, n.10, pp.14-15.

1938
"Proekt 'Bol'sogo Arteka'." ("'Grande Artek' Project.") *Arkhitektura Sssr*, n.10, pp.61-63.

98 **1929**
Jalovkin, F. "Zametka v svjazi e proektom U. Leonidova." ("Notes on I. Leonidov's Centrosoyuz project.") *Sovremennaya Arkhitektura,* n.2, pp.43-45.

1930
Kuz'min, A. "Protiv bezotvetsvennoj kritiki, K napadkam na proekty I. Leonidova." ("Against irresponsible criticism. On the attacks on projects of I. Leonidov.") *Sovremennaya Arkhitektura,* n.4, p.9.

Mordvinov, A.G. "Leonidovscina i e 'cred'." ("Leonidovism and its 'misdeeds'.") *Iskusstvo v Massy,* n.12.

Sovremennaya Arkhitektura, n.5, pp.2-5. Editorial on the Palace of Culture.

1931
"Rezoljueija sekcij Izo instituta Lija Kmakademj po dodlady T. Mordvinova 'O melkoburzuaznov napravlenij v architekture' ('leonidoscina'), prinjataja 20/7/1930." ("Resolution of the Izo section of the Lija Institute on the report: "The petit-bourgeois direction in architecture. ('Leonidovism'), published July 20, 1930.") *Sovetskaya Arkhitektura,* n.1-2, p.18.

"Rezoljucija obseego sobtanija sektora architektorov socialistic-eskogo strojtel'stva pri Vano po dokladu o tak nazyvaemoy 'leon-idovscine'." ("Resolution of the general assembly of the architects' sector of the socialist building near the Vano on the relation to the so-called 'Leonidovism'.") *Sovetskaya Arkhitektura,* n.1-2, p.102.

1934
Khiger, R. "Mastera molodoj architektury, A. Vlasov, I. Leonidov, M. Barsc, M. Sinjavskij." ("Masters of the young architecture: A. Vlasov, I. Leonidov, M. Barsc, M. Sinjavskij.") *Arkhitektura Sssr,* n.9, pp.33-38.

1963
Ju, Il'in-Adaev. "I.I. Leonidov." *Mosproektovec* (Jan. 1).

1964
Khan-Magomedov, S. "Ivan Leonidov." *Sovetskaya Arkhitektura, n.16, pp.103-116.*

1967
Khan-Magomedov, S. "Kluby Leonidova." ("The clubs of Leonidov.") *Dekorativnoye Iskusstvo Sssr,* n.11, pp.17-22.

1968
Aleksandrov, P. "I.I. Leonidov—architektor-novator." ("I.I. Leonidov—innovative architect.") *Arkhitektura Sssr,* n.1, pp.31-42.

1970
Kopp, A. *Town and Revolution: Soviet Architecture and City Planning 1917-1935.* New York: George Braziller, Inc.

"Progetto dell'Istituto Lenin: Architetto Ivan Leonidov." ("Lenin Institute Project: Architect Ivan Leonidov.") *L'Architettura: Cronache e Storia,* v.15, n.12, pp.834-836.

1971
Khan-Magomedov, S. "I.I. Leonidov 1902-1959." in *Building in the USSR 1917-1932.* Edited by O.A. Shvidkovsky. New York: Praeger Publishers, pp.124-128.

Khazanova, V. "Soviet Architectural Associations 1917-1932." in *Building in the USSR 1917-1932, pp.19-25.*

1973
Hrüza, Jirí. "Ivan Leonidov." *Architektura CSR,* v.32, n.5, pp.229-236. (Brief English summary, p.247.)

Hrüza, Jirí., and Kroha, Jirí. *Sovetská architektonická avant-garda.* Odeon.

1975
Quilici, Vieri, and Scolari, Massimo, eds. *Ivan Leonidov.* Milan: Franco Angeli Editore.

Bohigas, Oriol. "Los proyectos de Leonidov, el 'Leonidovismo' y la revisión historiográfica de Aledsandrov y Khan-Magomedov." ("The projects of Leonidov, 'Leonidovism' and Aleksandrov and Khan-Magomedov's historiographic revision.") *Arquitecturas Bis,* n.9, pp.1-5. Book review.

1978
Huxtable, Ada Louise. Review of IAUS exhibition entitled, "Ivan Leonidov: A Russian Visionary Architect 1902-1959." *New York Times,* February 12, Section 2, p.9, column 1.

1979
Cohen, Jean-Louis, Michelis, Marco, Tafuri, Manfredo, eds. *URSS 1917-1978: La Ville, L'Architecture.* Paris: L'Equerre.